# ZEN HOUSE RULES

## The busy mom's handbook for a healthier happier family home

Written by:
Dr. Terra Johnston, PhD

Published by:
Shore Stone Publishing
2022

## ABOUT THE BOOK

Written for the busy working mom, Zen House Rules translates the science of wellness into 8 easy steps. Outfox family stress, restore harmony in your home, parent with confidence, and nurture mind-body health for you and your loved ones. With evidence-based tools and tips, Zen House Rules are easy to follow, with proven staying power.

# ABOUT THE AUTHOR

Dr. Terra Johnston, PhD, is an expert research translator in the fields of mental health, addictions, childcare, and children's development. Following her fire-fighter husband's diagnosis with PTSD, Terra activated the science of wellness to restore harmony in her own family home. By weaving personal experiences with evidence-based discoveries in mind-body health, Terra's practical guidance is easy to follow and apply. As Founder of the Chalet Point Retreat Centre, Terra provides wellness education and training to a growing clientele of women leaders and professionals. Contact Terra at: terra@chaletpoint.ca.

# DISCLAIMER

This book is meant to spark interest in the science of mind-body health and wellness. It is not meant to diagnose or treat mental illness or health issues. Always consult with your healthcare professional before making changes to your health and psychological wellness routine.

# A NOTE OF CAUTION

During a meet-up for coffee with a friend of a friend—
let's call her Jane—a woman shared with me her most tightly
held secret: she was in an abusive relationship. Jane reached
out to me because she knew of my husband's experience with
PTSD. Her husband, as she explained, also struggled with
PTSD, and she was worried that his episodes of rage were
growing more and more violent. After listening to her story, I
encouraged her to seek professional help—both for him and
for her. Jane's husband was prone to violent behaviour. While
he had not hit her, he had punched the wall near Jane's head
and had damaged their property. She was worried he might
hurt himself. I was worried he might hurt Jane. I implored Jane
to put her own health and safety first. Hopefully, as I explained
to her, Jane's husband would be willing to receive professional
help as well, but until such time, she needed to take
immediate precautions to ensure her safety.

I'm happy to report that Jane did seek therapy; her husband, however, has yet to receive professional help and they continue to live apart. One day, I hope Jane's husband does reach out for help. But that will be his choice; one not even Jane can lead him to choose. If your situation is similar to Jane's—if your loved one is violent, self-harms, or threatens violence or self-harm—I implore you to put your safety first and to seek professional help.

# PREFACE

This book is not a comprehensive atlas on the science of wellness. There are many of those on the market, with technical explanations on the biomechanics of the brain, the gut, the autonomic nervous system, and the complex ways in which these bodily systems work together to respond to stress and activate our immune systems. And there are also many in-depth explorations into the science of mindfulness meditation and the cycles of motivation—science-heavy texts that delve deep into technical explanations. Instead, this book is a synthesis of the science of wellness; a bringing together of this complicated knowledge, to make sense of it and demonstrate how it can be used in practice to enhance our mind-body health.

Informed by evidence, this book translates complicated jargon to give you a solid understanding of the science of mental health and wellness.

For those of you whose curiosity has been sparked to dive deeper into this science, I encourage you to do so and provide recommendations for additional reading in the final chapter. For those of you who are coping with enormous family stress and the health struggles that accompany it, know this: I've been there. I know you need straightforward advice, informed by scientific evidence, that you can easily apply to restore health and happiness in your home. When life is busy, and family stress leaves you struggling to keep your head above water, you don't have the time or the resolve to delve into science-heavy reading. What you really need is a research translator—someone you can trust, someone who has also walked the journey you are on, someone who has personal experience in restoring health and happiness in the family home. I am that person. I have walked that journey. I have lived that experience. With my PhD-training in mental health research, I've done the homework for you so you can get on with the business of restoring your family's health and wellness and living your best life.

# DEDICATION

For David, who left us too soon, but will forever be part of our family.

# TABLE OF CONTENTS

# INTRODUCTION

*My personal awakening*

I am uncomfortable with profiling myself as an expert. Only experts write advice books, so claiming myself to be one has never sat right with me. But recently I was inspired to think differently about the role of expert. I was listening to an author talk about her childhood experiences and how the circumstances of her upbringing gave her a unique expertise that she wanted to share with others. I like that. That sits right with me. In my interpretation of the role of expert, it doesn't mean I believe myself to be an expert of all things, for all eternity. It more simply means that I have an expert knowledge, acquired by a unique set of events, in a particular area of life. That's me; that's what I bring to the table. I have most certainly lived through a unique set of events. So, with this important preface acknowledged up front, I proudly hold myself up as an expert in resilience and healing.

I have lived through a deep and dark depression brought on by multiple miscarriages and struggles with infertility; the chronic illness of my first husband, David, and the impact of his death on our daughter, Maggie; and the near implosion of my second marriage to Tony, due to his struggle with mental illness. I know intimately the experience of succumbing to despair, living through the motions of a sad and lonely life, numbing oneself through food and alcohol, and losing sight of the joys in life.

I also know the experience of digging out of the darkness and discovering the pathway to happiness and health. It is not my constitution, my grit, or some innate fortitude that makes me an expert on resilience and healing. It is my lived experience. And these experiences have been spectacular—I've got to say. I own them all, the dark ones, especially. In this way, I am proud to call myself an expert on resilience and healing, and it is my privilege to share my journey with you.

While I am a PhD-trained research translator in the fields of mental health, addictions, childcare, and children's development, the guidance I offer comes from the ups and downs of my personal journey toward health and wellness. A transformative event in my life was the near unraveling of my second marriage resulting from Tony's undiagnosed post-traumatic stress disorder (PTSD). Toward the end of a two-year recovery period, including months of expensive psychotherapy, my husband's progress seemingly stalled. It was frustrating for him, for me, and for our family. Not knowing what else to do or who else to approach for help and guidance, I did the only thing I knew how to do. I tackled his mental illness with my researcher's approach to problem-solving. I collected data on his stress triggers, gathered evidence to better understand the biomechanics of his anger-response patterns, and delved deep into the science of mind-body health.

Using this knowledge, I nudged my family toward a healthier lifestyle. I implemented slow and steady changes in our household, from diet and nutrition, exercise, mindfulness meditation, sleep hygiene, and positive reframing. The science of wellness transformed my family home. It can help yours, too.

This is my story…

Six years ago, I had an awakening. It was brought on by my husband Tony's mental health crisis. Tony acquired PTSD from the continuous exposure to the trauma he faced in his job of thirty years as a firefighter and Captain with the Winnipeg Fire Paramedic Department. Through the journey of Tony's recovery from PTSD, I became a reluctant expert on the disorder. PTSD moved into our house and the only way I could fight it was to study its make-up, learn its weaknesses, and outsmart its evil genius.  And wouldn't you know it? I did.

But it was the hardest thing I have ever done. To say Tony and I are stronger and more in love than ever before would be a half-truth. We are stronger, certainly. And there are lots of times when we are over the moon with joy. But our marriage has been redefined by Tony's PTSD experience. It is not his fault. It is not my fault. It is just our new normal. You see, the thing we experts in PTSD know, and know well, is that you can never turn your back on PTSD. It is always there, lurking, like a predator shark, just beneath the surface. As the partner of someone with PTSD, I know how dark the dark can be. I've seen it reflected in the eyes of my husband. And I know the terror of PTSD. I've seen its rage etched across his face. Yes, I know PTSD all too well—and I hate it with every atom of my being.

To say I never saw PTSD coming is both my truth and my shame. To be a trained and knowledgeable mental health research translator and not see the warning signs that were before my very eyes fills me with remorse. I completely missed the early signs of Tony's mental illness. I was, to be honest, pre-occupied with his physical health and safety. As a firefighter in the city of Winnipeg, Manitoba, Tony and his team of first responders were just that: first to respond, no matter the call. Fire? Check. Fire was to be expected of course, that was what he signed up to fight. Motor vehicle accidents, too, were not unexpected. But the suicides, attempted suicides, overdoses, street violence, homicides, domestic violence—the degree and volume of trauma that filled his every workday could never have been imagined or prepared for.

To better understand my obliviousness to Tony's simmering PTSD symptoms, it should be noted that his trauma-filled workdays were mostly hidden from me. Tony, as first responders commonly do, protected me from the psychological perils of the job. He let me worry about his sleeping schedule, or lack thereof, and the sky-reaching heights he faced amid the city's blazing rooftops, in the bucket of his engine truck. Never, though, would he tell me about the living nightmares he tended to, day in and day out. For thirty years, the violence, death, and pain he witnessed and experienced, not simply as a bystander (which would surely be enough to traumatize anyone), but as an active and immersed participant, were his norm, not the exception. Until one day he couldn't hide this trauma from me any longer.

That day was May 6, 2016. And it is a day that changed my life, my marriage, and my family forever. That day delineates my life as "before-PTSD" and "after-PTSD". And, while I marvel at the memories of my before-PTSD life, baffled by my carefree thinking and the naive trust I placed in the notion of a happy-ever-after, I have made peace with my after-PTSD world. I have learned to live with insecurity, the ever-present possibility that a bolt of lightning could strike my family home out of nowhere. "After-PTSD" is my new normal. It is a life I would never have chosen. And, still, it is a gift I would never return. It has led me here, many years into a journey that has revealed to me a mountain of wisdom that I would otherwise never have climbed. It is from this vantage point that I can take someone's hand when they are drowning in the dark pool of despair and say to them, with certainty: it will be okay.

In the first phase of Tony's recovery, his health and wellness became all-consuming for me. And after two years of this, it simply became too much for me. It was as though in my efforts to save Tony I slowly but steadily absorbed his pain and the stresses of his life. I became immensely unhappy, unfulfilled, exhausted, and desperately lonely. Eventually, as is the cycle of despair, this darkness began to leak out of me in the form of anger.

"What are you mad about now, mom?" my daughter would ask of me, more and more frequently. This crushed me. Not only did I not know why I was so angry, I found I couldn't stop my emotional outbursts. Anger, it seemed, was my new normal, and I worried about the example I was setting for my girl.

On top of that, like so many women, I was caught up in the whole perfect mother/perfect wife facade, and I felt I had no one to talk to about my despair. I had lost my partner and best friend—I felt I couldn't burden Tony with my own struggles while he fought for his life. And yet I knew I looked like I had everything under control to my friends, family, colleagues, and clients. They marveled at my ability to weather the storm I was in, and truth be told, I liked looking like I had it all together.

So, with this overblown ego-filled pride, there was no way I was going to expose to the world that I was falling apart on the inside. This inability to share truthfully and humbly with others is a common issue among women. I believe our desire to be viewed and valued as perfect (or, as near-perfect as womanly possible) is one of our greatest obstacles in life. And, quite frankly, I want to knock it down. I want to rid women of the soul-crushing pursuit of perfection. I believe that a support

system—one built on friendship, honesty, humility, and trust—
is the greatest gift we can possibly know.

This journey I'm on—and one that continues, to this
day—is my personal awakening. And I know I'm not done
growing and learning. I hope I continue to discover and
rediscover the lessons of life that I am meant to learn. Looking
back to that day on May 6, 2016, I have only self-compassion
for the woman I was then. I knew little of how to take care of
myself, to love myself, and to devote myself to living life in the
present. And I know I could only have learned these hard-
earned lessons the hard way. Six years ago, I had no choice
but to completely overhaul my life. Strip it down to the barest
of elements, and rebuild—slowly, but surely—a new approach
to being. I transformed my life's philosophy and my
understanding of what it means to be a woman, a wife, and a
mother. I shed my old, misplaced, and counterproductive
ideals of what I needed to be and who I needed to be. I shed
my anger and my worries, and I've never been happier.

Let me be clear, my life is not perfect. My husband
continues to live with a serious mental illness, and we struggle

with the ups and downs of this reality. Tony takes medications to keep his PTSD symptoms at bay, and sometimes these medications need to be reassessed and fine-tuned. As well, from time to time, Tony and I seek out couples counseling to help us work better as a team in our fight against his illness. Importantly, Tony is open and honest about his recovery journey; he shares his PTSD experience with other firefighters so that they will seek out help if they ever need it. I am awed by Tony's courage to combat the stigma associated with his mental illness. And his resolve to never give up in his fight against PTSD is a true testament to his strength. At the age of twenty-one, when Tony became a firefighter, he never imagined the toll his job choice would take on his health, his family and his life. As a young man, all Tony wanted was a career through which to help others—to be an everyday hero. And after thirty years of service, he was a hero to so many. In my eyes, he remains one to this day.

Statistically speaking, I know Tony and I are not alone. Over the course of a lifetime, 50% of Canadian adults will deal with a significant mental health crisis. With these odds, nearly every marriage in Canada has been or will be impacted by mental illness. But this reality doesn't mean our relationships are doomed. With good information and evidence-based wellness tools we can weather these storms in life. We can rebuild our marriages; we can restore our family homes; and we can turn our weaknesses into our greatest strengths. My family is proof of that.

CHAPTER 1

**Rule 1: Outfox family stress**

*Understand chronic stress and how it affects your family home*


We have grown accustomed to stress. Indeed, we see it as the inevitable by-product of modern society, just a normal part of our daily lives. We dismiss stress as a bothersome pest, ruining our picnic. True, it affects us all—there isn't a family home that is free from stress—but it is time for us to see stress for what it really is: the world's most deadly killer.


The state of health in contemporary society is dire: rates of anxiety, depression, obesity, and addiction have skyrocketed. Ground-breaking scientific research has pinpointed the root cause of this growing epidemic: chronic stress.

It has been estimated that over 80% of visits to the physician's office in the developed world are related to stress. When medical researchers examine today's leading causes of death, from cancer to cardiovascular disease to respiratory complications, they find stress at the root.  The health risks of chronic stress cannot be over-stated. Yet, still, we ignore its deadly effects. Why do we under-estimate the deadly power of chronic stress? And why do we over-estimate our power to conquer it?

Likely, because stress is so pervasive, we dismiss its effect on our health and happiness. Or, perhaps, the simpler explanation is that we ignore what we cannot see. Rather it is the symptoms of stress—disease, obesity, mental illness, and addictions—that capture our attention. Yet, all the while, stress continues its deadly work, unhampered, as we focus our efforts downstream, blind in our pursuit of symptom management.

Many of us fall victim to a culture of stress, believing in some twisted way that being over-stressed is the badge of productivity and achievement. Working mothers are a prime example. We love to commiserate with one another about the hectic pace of our busy lives and the never-ending challenge of work-home balance. Indeed, our over-stretched schedules are held up as proof that we are making the most of each day and giving our children every opportunity. The societal pressures on today's working moms have created a dangerous competition; we strive to outdo each other in the race to squeeze more busy-ness in our days. If this sounds familiar, it's imperative to recognize stress for what it really is: the biggest threat to your family home. But stress need not be the plight of the working mother. Nor should it be proof that you are living up to the demands of today's "more is more" culture. Make no mistake: the daily grind of chronic family stress is nothing to dismiss. But to take back the health and happiness of your family home, you must understand how stress works. Only then, will you be able to outfox it.

Today's stress has evolved from its early beginnings. Instead of the acute stressors faced by our ancient ancestors—being chased by a lion on the desert sands of the Serengeti, for example—we now have chronic stress. Work deadlines, parenting problems, credit card payments, house repairs, and overflowing laundry hampers—these are the new lions of modern life. And guess what? Our bodies treat these modern stressors the same way they treated those flesh and blood predators. Our bodily systems become activated into a state of "fight or flight"—our involuntary stress reaction—and rarely do we fully transition back to a healthy state of "rest and digest", the body's optimal state for recovery. The damage of chronic stress is all around us, as illustrated by these Canadian statistics.

- Mental Illness: According to the World Health Organization, depression is the second leading cause of disease. Youth are suffering too: 10-20% of Canadian youth are affected by mental illness, with a staggering 3.2 million youth at risk for developing depression.

- Poor Health: 62% of men and 46% of women are overweight or obese, putting them at great risk of cardiovascular disease and diabetes. Of Canadian youth, 30% are overweight or obese; a rate that has tripled in the last 30 years.

- Unhealthy Lifestyle Behaviours: Although it has decreased in the past ten years, 17% of Canadians continue to smoke tobacco, while 27% of men and 16% of women, ages 35-49 years, meet the criteria for heavy alcohol drinking. A mere 23% of men and 37% of women eat the daily recommended amounts of fruits and vegetables; and only 20% of adults and 10% of children meet Canada's recommended physical activity guidelines.

Depending on the headline of the day, it can be said that we have an obesity epidemic, a meth epidemic, or an anxiety epidemic. But, in actuality, we have a stress epidemic. Obesity, addictions, and mental illness—these are simply the symptoms of stress. When medical researchers explore the deaths related to chronic disease—such as cardiovascular disease, and deaths related to mental illness and addictions (often referred to as "deaths of despair")—they have discovered the underlying or indirect cause of these deaths to be chronic stress.

So how does stress get under our skin to negatively impact our biology? Well, to put it simply, the survival of our species is inextricably intertwined with our ability to recognize and respond to stress. The sympathetic response of our autonomic nervous system (fight or flight) is the key to our evolutionary success. And it is a perfect system for acute stress (immediate danger).

Through a complicated and involuntary system, we take in stress—we see it, sense it, taste it, hear it—and our sympathetic system springs into action. In times of threat, we need more energy in order to flee or fight the danger, so our blood sugar rises, our respiratory rate increases, and extra blood is pumped to our legs and arms. Our immune system also kicks in—and the resulting inflammation, a major byproduct of stress, is meant to cushion our organs from harm, such as the sharp sinking teeth of a charging lion. Then, once the acute stress is over, our parasympathetic system (rest and digest) kicks in and our bodily systems return to normal. Our blood pressure decreases, our heart rate relaxes, our blood sugar drops, and our immune system returns to homeostasis. In this calm state we enjoy a sense of safety, with an at-ease state of mind and bodily systems that work the way they should.

But chronic stress (persistent and prolonged stress) is a different beast. It keeps our bodies in constant fight-or-flight response and denies us the much-needed opportunity to return to a calm state of rest and digest. Our body's reaction to a predator on the Serengeti is the same as our reaction to the mounting overdue bills, or the pressing deadlines at work, or the dirty dishes piling up in the kitchen, or the conflict with our kids or spouses. Chronic stress triggers our sympathetic response—fight or flight—and it does not shut off. Aside from the heightened blood pressure, blood sugar, heart rate, and respiratory rate, we are also left with increased inflammation and an immune system that becomes so overactive that it loses its ability to be functional-specific. This leads to myriad stress-related health concerns, from auto-immune disorders to chronic fatigue, to cardiovascular disease. It can also lead to depression and anxiety.

To outfox family stress, it is important to remember that chronic stress is an unavoidable by-product of today's modern world. In other words, it is simply not possible to eliminate stress from your household. Rather, we must co-exist with stress through evidence-based approaches that mitigate their harms. Banishing stress from your life is not a sustainable approach to restoring harmony in your family home. In this way, stress should be thought of as an annoying houseguest that never leaves. It is here to stay. So, with this hard truth in mind, the question we must ask ourselves is: how do we coexist with stress?

While our fight or flight response is involuntary, there are proven ways to turn off our body's automatic fear reactions to stress. Key among these proven ways is mindfulness meditation.

Mindfulness meditation turns down our sympathetic nervous system and activates our parasympathetic nervous system. And, when we are no longer in fight or flight response, we can take back control of our involuntary nervous system and return to a calm state of mind.

So how do we make mindfulness meditation a long-lasting healthy habit? We'll get to that in rule 2: upgrade your brain. First, we must develop an ability to see the fight or flight responses that happen each and every day in your family home. In essence, we need to develop *stress-ray vision*. While it may sound simple enough, make no mistake, the ability to spot stress is a superpower. With stress-ray vision you can create a healthier and happier family home for you and your loved ones.

To develop stress-ray vision, you will need to take on a new identity, that of a field researcher or ethnographer. In social research terms, an ethnographer becomes immersed in her research study. A perfect example of this is Dr. Jane Goodall, who studied her beloved gorillas. Dr. Goodall lived among her research subjects, participated in their daily lives and traditions, and—importantly—took copious notes in her study. Adopting the role of a field researcher will remove you from taking on the emotional ups and downs of your loved ones. This healthy detachment will enable you to "zoom out" so that you can observe the stress responses in your family home without succumbing to them yourself.

Start by getting a notebook that you will dedicate to your research—and keep it confidential and tucked away from prying eyes (a pocket-sized notebook is great, or a note-taking app on your smart phone works well, too).

This notebook is for your field notes—a research tool where you will record what you observe. Through the conscious act of taking field notes, you will become more observant of the often-missed flight or fight responses of your loved ones that occur in their response to daily chronic stress. A dedicated notebook will allow you to keep track of the common stressors in your household and your family's general reactions to these stressors. However, before you record your observations of your loved ones and their reactions to chronic stress, you will need to spend some time observing and recording your own fight or flight responses to the stressors in your life. Here's an example of what this might look like:

| My stressors | My stress responses |
|---|---|
| Maggie couldn't find her gym shoes for school; I didn't sleep well and feel sluggish and cranky. | I yelled at Maggie and accused her of being careless with her belongings; I drank way too much coffee and over-ate throughout the day; I was not productive at work. |
| Tony was officer-in-command at a large apartment fire, and I worried all night about him. | I had a terrible sleep, called in sick for work and ended up binging on Netflix all day. |
| I was behind on a work deadline and had to take work home with me to catch up; Maggie wanted me to bake cookies in the evening, but I didn't have time. | I felt like a terrible mother and a terrible employee; I drank too much wine. |
| Tony was on his day off and forgot to run the errand I asked him to. | I over-reacted to Tony's forgetfulness and we had a big fight. |
| The weekend was very busy, so I had to stay up late on Sunday night to do laundry. | I yelled at Maggie about her messy room. |

Once you have spent a couple weeks tracking your own stressors and your fight or flight responses, you can progress into stealthy research-mode and study the stressors and responses of your loved ones. The following is an example of how to track and monitor the stressors and stress responses of your family:

| My family's stressors | My family's stress responses |
|---|---|
| Mornings are chaotic and busy, especially Monday mornings. I worried about getting Maggie to school on time and getting myself to work on time. | I yelled at Maggie to hurry up; I felt she didn't listen to me, so I yelled louder. Maggie yelled back at me, stormed off to her room and zoned out on her smart phone (and we were, of course, late for school and work). |
| Tony forgot about weekend plans to attend my family gathering. I felt ignored and unimportant to him. | When I told Tony that I was upset with him for forgetting our family gathering, he yelled at me for not being a supportive wife. We got into a big fight and he slept in the spare bedroom. |
| Tony got upset about the heating bill and yelled at Maggie for leaving her space heater on in her bedroom. | Maggie cried and ran to her room. I yelled at Tony for being mean to Maggie. We all spent the evening apart watching TV in our separate spaces. |

In the example of these field notes you may have noticed a "freeze" response (I called in sick to work and binged on Netflix all day; Maggie zoned out on her smart phone). There is growing acceptance that in addition to our body's fight or flight response, a freeze response is also a common stress response of our sympathetic nervous system. A freeze response may look passive; indeed, it may even appear as though a person is unaffected by a stressor. But importantly, a freeze response should be viewed as a stress response and responded to as such—with patience and kindness. In this way, a freeze response warrants the same approach as the body's fight or flight response. You cannot yell at it and expect it to go away. Just as it would be illogical to expect a person's involuntary sympathetic nervous system to immediately deactivate and their parasympathetic nervous system to immediately activate (the shift from fight or flight to rest and digest), we must also be patient with the freeze response. Recognizing the different ways by which we and our loved ones exhibit the activation of our sympathetic nervous systems is key to developing stress-ray vision. We do not all respond to stress in the same manner. Some of us yell and scream (fight), some of storm off (flight), and some of us withdraw (freeze). The stress response of your loved ones will look different from your own and from each other's.

From time to time, my husband's PTSD will rear its ugly head and turn my gentle-tempered husband into a grizzly bear. Often, he has little insight into what triggers him. But I do—now. I collected my data and became an expert on the types of stress that are triggers for him. From the vantage point of stealthy field researcher, I approached his dark moods with a calm objectivity. And this calm objectivity is now my superpower.

But I didn't always have stress-ray vision. Quite the contrary. Before, I would get easily offended by a sharp or critical tone, especially if it was delivered by my husband.

And whenever I felt wronged, I would demand to work through the injustice, blind in my conviction that I could talk reason to him when he was so clearly not in a reasonable frame of mind. I know now that when Tony is in a dark mood, his fight reaction is activated and his limbic system (nestled within his less-evolved, mammalian brain) is doing all the so-called thinking. Understanding the biomechanics of his inner brain demystifies his outburst for me. And while his limbic system is in charge of his thinking, I know there is no point in reasoning with him. It is simply not the right time.

I think of stress-ray vision as a calm objectivity that allows me to slow down the world and my reactions to it. Remember Neo, Keanu Reeve's character from the Matrix? Well, that's who I become. Whenever Tony lobs a sharp tone or unfair criticism at me, I become Neo in the scene where his world slows down and he fights the bad guy (chronic stress) in a one-arm-behind-the-back sort of way.

Just like Neo, the pace of my world slows down and the biomechanics of Tony's dark mood become revealed to me. I see through his anger, like the streams of green code in the Matrix, and I decode his anger to reveal the fight response that lies beneath. I see his blood pumping, his heart racing, and his breathing elevated. And so, I meet his sharp tone with calm control; I deflect it, with one hand behind my back. His dark moods, or sharp tones, or unfair criticisms are not allowed into my sphere; his anger cannot penetrate me. I become the field researcher, healthily detached and calmly objective.

It's important to understand that calm objectivity is not a wall of indifference that I have erected between me and my spouse. Rather, through my understanding of Tony's PTSD and the scientific knowledge of his body's response to fear, I now know—both in my head and in my heart—that his anger is not about me.

I am simply his closest target, and his angry words are not mine to absorb. I'm in charge of my emotions and my reactions, and my self-worth; indeed, my own health and happiness, are not dictated by him—or by anyone else, for that matter. The love I have for myself and the trust I place in my inherent goodness are not given to me by anyone; nor can they be taken away by anyone. It is this understanding that sets the foundation to the happiness and health of my family home.

When Tony's PTSD gets the better of him and he blows off steam, his limbic system takes over his pre-frontal cortex, the part of his brain in charge of executive functioning and reason. And, because of his exposure to trauma, his limbic system is especially fragile: trauma has impaired his amygdala, the brain's emotional regulation system.

Only when he calms down can we enter a space of reconciliation. And it happens, as I've discovered. Once his fight or flight response turns off, Tony comes back to me, humble and apologetic, and we move forward. Don't get me wrong, he does not get a free pass to be an asshole to me or our daughter anytime he feels like it. But, like all people who live with mental illness, recovery is a journey and relapses are par for the course. Punishing or cold-shouldering Tony so he feels guilty or remorseful for his mistakes is a no-win game. One day, I know Tony will kick his PTSD for good, and I know it's just a matter of time before he fully repairs the damage done to his brain by the trauma to which it was exposed.

Conducting household research on your and your family's fight or flight (or freeze) responses to the daily stressors in your family home will give you important knowledge upon which to develop ways to manage the effects of stress on you and your loved ones. Remember, chronic stress is an inevitable by-product of our modern world. While it may be tempting to think we can banish stress from our lives and protect our loved ones from its damaging consequences, it is not a sustainable approach to a healthier and happier life. Chronic stress is that houseguest that refuses to leave and we must learn to co-exist with it and diminish its harmful impact on our health and mental health.

By conducting important field research in your family home, you will gain stress-ray vision. This stress-ray vision will lead you toward calm objectivity, allowing you to remain healthily detached from the stress responses of your loved ones when they react to the daily stressors of life. And you will also discover a newfound empathy for your loved ones. Rather than becoming irritated by your child's outburst (fight) or your partner's withdrawal (freeze), you will learn to interpret their outbursts as their body's involuntary reaction to stress. And, importantly you will learn not to equate their unpleasant reaction to stress as a failure of their character. Rather, you will see their negative behaviour for what it really is—an involuntary response to stress.

As you might imagine, gaining stress-ray vision will prepare you to anticipate predictable stressors in your life and better cope with those surprise stressors that disrupt your life. Stress-ray vision will also help you react to the negative behaviours of your loved ones with greater empathy, understanding, and calmness. With stress-ray vision, you can rise above your spouse's anger response to an unexpected financial stressor when the dishwasher breaks down. And you can give him the space he needs to deactivate his sympathetic nervous system and safely recover from his stress response.

Once his fight response is deactivated and his ability to think and act rationally returns, then—and only then—will you be able to discuss how to best deal with the stressor at hand. By not engaging with him while he is in his fight response, you are preventing further stress from exacerbating his fight response (the added stress of a marital dispute—a so-called bonus to the original stressor), which will help him deactivate his stress response quicker.

Further, by disengaging from his fight response, you will protect your own state of wellness. His stress response does not have to trigger a stress response in you. You can be the gatekeeper to your emotions, protecting and prioritizing your state of calmness over his fight response. As you grow in your ability to combat stress with calm objectivity, you will grow more empathetic and patient with your loved ones as you remind yourself that their negative behavior is not a flaw of their character.

You will more easily recall their positive qualities and see their negative behaviours as just ineffective stress responses. In this way, their ineffective stress responses become the target of your interventions—you do not need to 'fix' their character. Rather, you will shift toward teaching them, through the patience and calm objectivity, how to better handle their stress (the focus of the next rule: upgrade your brain) and you will develop stress mitigation strategies to help alleviate the impacts of their stressors.

Let's go back to the example of my field notes. Here's how I developed a plan to support my loved ones to learn and apply healthier ways to mitigate their stressors.

| My family's stressors | My mitigation strategies |
| --- | --- |
| Chaotic and busy schedules | I will wake up 15 minutes earlier so I can meditate before the chaos begins. I will remind myself, out loud, to stay calm and not yell. I will give Maggie one directive at a time so as not to overwhelm her with too many demands at once. I will play happy upbeat music during our morning routine to set the stage for a positive day. |
| Marital conflict | When I feel ignored by Tony, I will not react in anger; rather, I will journal my thoughts and, when I feel more in control of my feelings, I will find a time when I can calmly express my insecurity to him. |
| Financial worry | When Tony is triggered by financial worry, I will not react to his anger. Instead, I will calmly tell him that I am happy to review our family budget when he is in a calmer state of mind. |

You might be asking yourselves if these mitigation strategies are band-aid solutions to the negative stress responses of your loved ones. Well, sort of—but only if you stop here. Moving forward, I will show you how you can help your loved ones to turn off their fight, flight or freeze responses so that they do not have to rely on you and your newfound savvy for outfoxing household stress. These techniques are found in the next chapter, rule 2: upgrade your brain.

CHAPTER 2

**Rule 2: Upgrade your brain**

*Activate cost-free tools to enhance mind-body health*

The statistics are dire. In any given year, 1 in 5 Canadians experience a mental illness or addiction problem. By the time Canadians reach 40 years of age, 1 in 2 will have experienced a mental illness or addiction problem. Mental illness is the leading cause of disability in Canada. People with mental illness and addiction problems are more likely to die prematurely than the general population. Mental illness can cut 10 to 20 years from a person's life expectancy.

These are some hard truths, but the point of sharing these statistics is to demonstrate the urgent need to value and protect our mental health as though our life depends on it (and it does).

So how do we do this? If we look to the science of wellness there is no better foundation to positive mental health than a daily practice of mindfulness meditation. But for many of us, meditation seems too good to be true. I, too, was skeptical. But once I explored the scientific evidence behind mindfulness meditation, I was hooked.

Mindfulness meditation is getting a lot of buzz and attention recently, but this wellness tool is not new—indeed, it is 2500 years old. Now, through modern medical technology, neurobiologists have discovered the ways by which mindfulness meditation changes our brain structure. This research demonstrates how mindfulness meditation increases our grey matter, which can, in turn, reduce the effects of aging on the brain. It also increases the capacity of our hippocampus, which improves the way we handle emotions such as fear, anger, and sadness.

Mindfulness meditation also activates our left prefrontal cortex, which leads to happier moods. The list of benefits goes on and on; but in essence, a meditative brain is a healthier, happier brain.

Before we get into the "how-to" of mindfulness meditation, here are a few key concepts that will help you better understand how and why it works. Brain imaging shows how mindfulness meditation changes our brain functioning so that we are better wired to handle the difficult emotions that come from a steady diet of chronic stress. Yet, despite the irrefutable proof of this stress management tool—and its zero-cost price tag—few people integrate mindfulness meditation into their daily routines. With an understanding of how it works, I believe mindfulness meditation can become a wellness tool each of us, from children to seniors, can commit to daily.

Mindfulness meditation helps us to deal with chronic stress by turning down our sympathetic nervous system and activating our parasympathetic nervous system. When we are no longer in fight, flight, or freeze mode, we can take back control of our involuntary nervous system and make smarter, healthier choices in all aspects of our lives. Scientific studies demonstrate that mindfulness meditation changes the brain, specifically the parts associated with emotional regulation and cognitive functioning. Using high-resolution scans of the brain, mindfulness meditation is shown to increase grey matter in several key areas of the brain, including the hippocampus, the posterior cingulate cortex, the left temporoparietal junction and the cerebellum.

Simply put, the more grey matter we have in our brain, the more neurons it has. And the more neurons we have in our brain, the better it functions.

An increase in the grey matter of our hippocampus is especially good news; this is the area of the brain associated with emotional regulation and our ability to turn down our fight-flight-freeze responses to stress. As I've said, there are great resources that explain the nature of the brain and the different components that regulate different functions, such as memory, language, body movement, and arousal. I have included several of these for your reference in the final chapter. If you are a skeptic of mindfulness meditation, you may want to explore these resources; sometimes a thorough understanding of the science behind a wellness tool is needed before one can fully commit to it. However, while the scientific explanation of mindfulness meditation exists, it is not a pre-requisite to using it. Just as I know nothing about how my car engine works, I know how to drive my car and I know the benefits it brings to my life. My not being able to change my engine oil by myself should not be an obstacle to driving my vehicle. And, for busy readers such as yourself, not having the time to explore the biological underpinnings of the brain and the mechanics of brain scan imaging should not prevent you from benefiting from the increased grey matter your brain will achieve through a steady diet of mindfulness meditation.

When I discuss mindfulness meditation with my clients, family members and friends, nearly everyone tells me the same thing: I suck at meditating. If you are thinking the same thing, let me tell you what I tell them. If you can breathe, you can meditate. The people I speak with tell me they are worried that they are "doing it wrong", or that when they try to meditate they end up with wandering minds. But that's exactly what meditation is: it's trying to concentrate, noticing your mind wander, and bringing it back—without judgement—to concentration.

One way I explain the technique and benefit of mindfulness meditation is by using a weight training analogy.

My husband lifts weights, so this analogy has been helpful for him. The point of weightlifting is to push your muscles to the point of exhaustion—or in the case of mindfulness meditation, to the point of distraction. In other words, mindfulness meditation is not supposed to be easy, just like weightlifting is not supposed to be easy. No pain, no gain, right? And just like we celebrate completing a tough weight training workout, so, too, should we celebrate our ability to stick to a tough meditation session. We would never dismiss a workout for being too difficult; rather, we bask in the accomplishment of pushing through an especially tough session. By extension, if meditation is difficult for you, celebrate your discipline and resolve to tackle the activity—do not expect it to be easy, and do not admonish yourself for experiencing difficulty.

The other important consideration of mindfulness meditation is that the process of noticing your mind wander is a good thing. In fact, it's actually the main point of meditation.

When your mind wanders, you are not failing at mindfulness meditation. Quite the contrary. When your mind wanders, it provides you with the opportunity to notice the distracted mind and—this is the important part—*gently* bring it back to focus. When I say gently, I mean the voice in your head should be gentle and kind. That gentle inner monologue might go something like this:

*As I'm concentrating on my breathing, I bring my attention to the rise of my belly as I inhale. When I slowly exhale, I bring my attention to the fall of my belly as I contract my diaphragm. Soon I notice my mind begins to think about the time (How much time has passed since I started? What will I make for dinner tonight? What is that smell coming from the kitchen? Did I send that email that was due today?). In a kind and nurturing way, I acknowledge my distracted mind. I tell it, you are OK, you are meditating for your mind-body health, let the distraction go.*

Notice in this example, I do not scold myself for letting my mind wander. I do not think "I suck at meditation". Instead, I am kind to myself. I detach from my mind as though it is a restless toddler, running from thought to thought. Instead of being annoyed at my toddler mind, I take her by the hand and in a warm and loving way I say, "it's OK, come back to me, let's try again". And this is the whole point of mindfulness meditation: to become a non-judgmental observer of oneself and others.

Once you begin to notice how the mind roams, you are becoming aware of your thinking and your thoughts. Most often, especially in today's hectic lifestyle, we operate on autopilot and the steady stream of thoughts in our mind leap from one worry to the next. For most of us, we don't even realize the critical voice inside our head that judges our every misstep.

We blindly accept it as the norm. But through mindfulness meditation, we start to notice our distracted toddler mind and our runaway thoughts, and—most importantly—we recognize our critical inner voice and recalibrate it to be gentle and kind. Take a moment here and think about the voice in your head. When you are disappointed by something that didn't go your way at work, what does the voice in your head sound like? What does the voice say? If the inner voice in your head is critical, it might tell you that you are never going to be the perfect employee or the perfect mother. Likely, this critical inner soundtrack is on a never-ending loop, playing in the background completely unnoticed, like ambient negative talk. When you begin to practice mindfulness meditation, you will become more aware of that voice in your head. And, with repeated practice, you will train that voice to be softer, gentler, and kinder.

The "doing" of mindfulness meditation is called "practice". And rightly so. Even the most experienced meditators still "practice" meditation. It is a lifelong process of learning, discovering, relearning, and rediscovering. If you are just starting out in your practice of mindfulness meditation, I encourage you to stick with a daily commitment of just a few minutes a day. Consistency is key here; it is far more important to meditate for short but frequent sessions versus long but sporadic sessions. Start with meditation practices of one minute, sprinkled throughout your day (before or after meals, is a great way to ensure three sessions per day).

Mindfulness meditation encompasses three things: concentration to focus the mind; open monitoring which helps us notice how our mind wanders and hear the (critical?) voice in our head; and acceptance practices (loving kindness) which bring comfort to us.

A main difference between mindfulness meditation and other psychological treatments (e.g., talk therapy) is its focus on understanding our thoughts and cultivating a different relationship with our thoughts. Non-judgmental acceptance is imperative for this. We cultivate non-judgmental acceptance by paying attention to our critical mind, those judgments about ourselves and others. But importantly, we do not try to banish these critical thoughts. Instead, we simply recognize them, as though we are holding the thoughts in our hands, one by one, as they pop into focus. We examine the passing critical thought, we turn it around, this way and that, and then we let it go, dropping it into the metaphorical bucket. Through this practice we begin to see ourselves and others more clearly. We begin to accept our own imperfections and we become more accepting of others and their imperfections. Self-acceptance and compassion are the goals for this Zen House Rule. And once we grow in our ability to be compassionate and accepting of ourselves and of others, we can model this way of being for our spouse, our children, and our loved ones.

Through consistent mindfulness meditation practice, you will notice the trouble with your thoughts—how they can be negative, paranoid, impatient, and even cruel. By understanding your thoughts, you can then begin to observe them from a place of detached observer. Just as we did in rule 1: outfox family stress, here, too, we become the field researcher of our minds. We pay attention to the noise, the critical voice, and the judgments we hold of ourselves and others. And we recognize that these thoughts are not always to be trusted; they are often—most often—the result of our critical self, our insecurities, and our fears.

For example, have you ever noticed how the love you feel for your partner can ebb and flow over the course of a week—maybe, sometimes, even throughout the day? How can it be that we love our spouse one day, but hate him the next?

When this happens to me, I know it's time to meditate. I know it's time to sit with my thoughts, hold them in my hands, examine them, and then let them go. I need to become a detached observer of my mind, to sit with myself and turn down my fight-flight-freeze response and activate my parasympathetic nervous system. I do this often, each and every day. Even if I can only find 5 minutes to practice, I ensure that I commit to a daily routine of mindfulness meditation. It has made me a calmer person, a more supportive partner, a more loving mother, and a better human being.  So how do you start?

I recommend starting with a deep belly breathing meditation. Find a quiet place (it's ok to tell your kids to leave you alone for a few minutes—indeed, its good role modeling for self-care); sit up straight in a chair (or lie down, if that's your preference); close your eyes; and place one hand on your belly.

Breath in deeply (through the nose, always breathe through the nose) and expand the belly, counting slowly to five. Exhale deeply and contract the belly, counting slowly to five, six or seven (whichever is most comfortable). Focusing on the expansion and contracting of your belly and counting the seconds of each inhale and exhale should focus your mind on the breath. But remember, when (not if) you notice your mind wandering, be gentle with yourself. Smile at your wandering toddler mind, take it by the hand and redirect it to the breath. It really is that simple.

Importantly, you can insert mindfulness meditation into your family's routine at many different opportunities. When you are stuck in traffic or in the grocery line, be grateful for the opportunity to practice a few deep belly breaths and lead your family in the practice.

When you are eating an apple, try mindful eating: take a bite of a crisp apple and observe the sound of the crunch and the jolt of the sugar on your tongue; chew slowly and when you swallow your bite of apple, imagine its journey as it makes its way into your blood stream. Take your kids on this adventure of mindful eating; make it a fun game for them, they'll love it.

Another tip to upgrading your brain is to make mindfulness meditation the first thing you do each and every day. I used to be a chronic snooze button-hitter. If I had to be up by 7:00 AM, I would set my alarm for 6:30 AM, and enjoy, as strange as it sounds, the state of my mind as I verged between sleep and wakefulness. Once I began to learn more about mindfulness meditation, I realized I could habit stack (a great way to build new healthy habits by piggybacking on existing habits) by incorporating mindfulness meditation into this early morning routine.

Now, instead of hitting the snooze button and drifting back into lucid dreaming, I meditate. I set my alarm clock 15 minutes before I need to wake up. Once my alarm sounds, I smile (the brain interprets our facial movements, so I smile to my brain to signal to it that I am happy to be awake). Then I place my right hand on my belly to help me remember to belly breathe. I inhale deeply (through my nose) and feel my belly and hand rise; and I exhale deeply and feel my belly and hand descend. I do this deep belly breathing for several minutes. Then I'm ready to transition to the next part of my early morning meditation practice, which is positive self-talk. I articulate in my head why I am grateful for the day. I take inventory of the assets I have in my life and I frame them through a positive lens—my body (I may no longer be young, but I am a healthy 50-year old), my home (it may need some reorganizing, but it's my safe haven and refuge), my work (I may be beholden to my deadlines and responsibilities, but my job affords me financial security), my family (even though we fight sometimes, I know they love me and I them), and my mind (I'm not perfect, but my goal is self-compassion, not perfection).

Next, I articulate how I will conduct myself throughout the day with positivity. I say in my head such things as, "today I will be generous in my support to my colleagues"; or "today I will be gentle with my daughter if she talks critically to me". I fully believe that by articulating my intentions to conduct myself positively I set myself up for a good day. And I also believe that this positive mindset is contagious. Try it for yourself and see how your loved ones react to your commitment to a positive way of being. My bet is they will follow suit.

There is a well-known family dinner custom of sharing the high points and the low points of one's day. Each family member takes a turn in telling the others about what happened to them at school, work, play, etc.

It's a great way to connect over the sharing of a meal. While I'm not suggesting to anyone that they abandon this custom, I would like to offer a second custom. You can do this over breakfast, or the drive to school and work (drives are perfect for this exercise; there is something about a car ride that makes conversation so much easier). One by one, have each family member discuss an event that is planned for them that day (perhaps you are leading a staff meeting, or your daughter is writing a difficult test). As you begin this new custom, go first and lead by example. It's important to model the type of positive self-talk that you would like your spouse or children to emulate. It might go something like this:

*This morning I am leading a staff meeting and I have developed an agenda to discuss how my team will divide tasks for an important project. When I introduce the new project, I will smile and describe how it will benefit the company. I will tell my team members that the project is a great opportunity to enhance our operations. I will nominate myself to take on a piece of the work that is difficult, to demonstrate to my team that I am willing and happy to contribute to the hard work involved. I will smile at my team members and encourage them to think about which tasks they want to take on. I will meet any criticism with positivity. If someone attempts to bring negativity into the meeting, I will deflect their attitude with a solution-focused attitude.*

The point of this practice is to demonstrate the how-to of positive self-talk to your spouse and your children. Then you can encourage your loved ones to try it themselves. Importantly, give them positive feedback on their first attempts at positive self-talk. Do not correct them or judge them (that defeats the purpose of nurturing that positive inner voice in their heads). Make this exercise fun; it's perfectly ok to be silly and laugh. I truly believe that starting your day on a positive note, collectively, as a family, is instrumental in nurturing the health and happiness of your family home.

CHAPTER 3

**Rule 3: Play for life**

*Apply the science of motivation for personal growth*

Most people have a linear definition of doing. You start something, you work at it, and then you finish. We tend to think of happiness the same way: we pursue happiness as though happiness itself is the end-goal.  We imagine that if we work hard in life, we will be rewarded with the golden years of retirement when we can finally put our feet up and enjoy a hard-earned rest. We have been conditioned to run to the finish line. But this implies that our reward comes at the end of the race.

And what is that reward, exactly? The promise of rest...but then what? The reward of rest doesn't sound all that exciting, does it?  But what if after we crossed that finish line, we kept on running?

We might then discover a deeper love for running, not because we have to run, but because we *want* to. Running because we want to run. Working because we want to work. Doing because we want to do. And growing because we want to grow. This is the wisdom we first knew as children, and it is the secret to a healthier, happier family home.

In the field of early childhood development, the theory of play-based learning acknowledges that children learn best through self-directed play. As children, we knew the importance of play in the pursuit of growing and mastering new skills. First, we crawled, then we toddled, eventually we walked, and before our parents could blink, we were running faster than they could catch us. But we didn't think of these steps toward our goal of running as "work"—we thought of them as play.

We all share the universal experience of learning to walk. We started off small, with baby steps. We fell. We got up. We fell again. We got up again. We took a helping hand when it was offered. We soaked up the cheers of support from our family. We kept at it, intrinsically determined and motivated to succeed. And although we did not succeed overnight, we were rewarded by the fun of it. Think of yourself as that child who learned to walk. What did you do next? I bet you did as all children do; you turned your sights to the next big challenge: climbing a hill, riding a bike, skipping a rope, and so on. As children, we thrived on conquering new obstacles, we enjoyed the act of practice, and we sought out new and increasingly challenging hurdles to master. This is the wisdom of childhood that we lost as we grew into adults.

So, what happened to this wisdom of childhood as we grew older?

As adults we've been conditioned to desire a hurdle-free life. We began to believe that happiness is the elimination of challenges and struggles. And in doing so, we lost something extremely precious: the desire to achieve new goals through the pursuit of personal growth. When we were children, play was always within reach. It was something we could do anytime, anywhere, any place. As grown-ups, we replaced play with a never-ending list of work, jobs, housework, and errands. We imagined what life might be like if only we were rich and could afford to hire someone to do our chores for us. The trouble with this fantasy is that it portrays happiness as a life that is hurdle-free, when in fact its life's hurdles and the pursuit of mastering these challenges that brings us the greatest joy. After all, haven't you noticed the miseries that fall upon the rich and famous? If money does indeed buy happiness, why do so many celebrities often fall into the traps of addiction, failed romance, and self-absorption? Money does not lead to happiness, nor does a hurdle-free life.

The wisdom of childhood provides us with a simple approach we can apply to any challenge in life we wish to master. First, we set a goal: something specific we wish to achieve. While people are quick to say they want healthier and happier lives, it is much harder to imagine what specific goals will lead to those healthier and happier outcomes. For example, rather than saying you wish you had less stress in your life, you might say you wish to grow your skills to better manage the stress in your life. While this re-wording might seem like a matter of semantics, reframing your goal into measurable and achievable steps provides you with a clearer and more manageable road map to steer you toward success. Plus, removing stress is often outside of our control; conversely, managing stress is within our control.

Second, we define our goal by incremental achievements or milestones. This is similar to the way our childhood goal of mobility was defined by the incremental achievements of crawling, toddling, walking, and running. In keeping with the example of wanting to grow your skills to better manage stress, your incremental achievements might include learning more about a stress management technique, such as mindfulness meditation. You might then commit to practicing mindfulness meditation just one minute of the day each morning of the work week (you could try the snooze button technique presented in rule 2: upgrade your brain). Next, you could try incorporating a longer meditation practice on the weekends, such as a 10-minute guided practice using one of many free meditation apps or audio recordings. Each week, slowly increase the number of times you meditate, aiming for three times a day of ten minutes each. Eventually, after several weeks, or even months, of this practice, you may work your way up to an intensive meditation experience, such as a full-day retreat.

That simple first step in mindfulness meditation is akin to crawling when you were a baby. A first step must be a manageable step, one that is achievable, and, from there, easy to build upon. The subsequent steps may grow in complexity, but they are, indeed, manageable if taken one by one.

The next phase of acquiring healthy habits is maintaining our motivation. This phase is when people often lose their commitment to their journey toward personal growth. But this phase need not be challenging, we can simply maintain our motivation by celebrating our incremental achievements just the way we soaked up the cheers from our families as we learned to take our first steps.

Creating moments to self-reflect and acknowledge our achievements is an important part of maintaining our momentum and building toward even greater success.

Such moments create ceremony in our life, the simple act of cherishing ourselves and honouring the courage and determination of our actions. Create a special time for yourself when celebrating your incremental achievements. Life is busy, certainly, but an important step to maintaining your motivation toward optimal personal growth is to honour your accomplishments. In creating a special time to celebrate these achievements, you are creating ceremony for yourself. Whether it be ten minutes or an hour, this ceremony is a significant demonstration, to both you and to your loved ones, that you value yourself and that you are dedicated to the pursuit of personal growth.

It is important to be positive in your self-reflection. Remember, you are celebrating your successes, no matter how small these incremental achievements may seem. Enjoy the process of mastering your challenges. Don't race to the finish line. Enjoy the struggle of hard work; success and happiness are sure to follow.

Here is an example of how to apply the wisdom of childhood through the pursuit of personal growth. I created this exercise for a client who came to me because she was restless, bored, and unhappy in her life. This example focuses on the pursuit of learning for personal growth, but you can apply the same principles to any aspect of your life in which you have an interest or a goal.

*The Goal of Learning for Personal Growth*

As a mother, you know the importance of reading to a child every day. But do you follow this same practice for yourself? If reading is not your strong suit, then reclaim your curiosity through documentaries. Discover something that you are passionate about and tackle it with gusto. There is a plethora of documentaries available on a range of interests from sport, travel, the environment, the economy, social welfare, and political issues.

Reclaim your curiosity and become an expert on an area—any area—of your choice. You'll soon discover an intellectual passion that brings you true and authentic joy.

Step 1: Reflect on your goal

Are you having difficulty tapping into your curiosity? Think back to your childhood. What did you enjoy doing? Here are some questions to help you identify your passions and ignite your curiosity:

-Where do you come from? Examine your genealogy roots and learn about the cultures and homelands of your ancestors.

-Where do you want to go? Are there places that you've always wanted to visit? Travel books and history books will help you discover the traditions and cultures of other lands. Or explore your own community—dig into the history of the buildings that surround you, investigate the biographies behind the names that adorn your neighbourhood parks and streets.

-Are you a sports or movie nut? Explore the biographies of your favourite stars or athletes.

-Interested in politics? There are tons of great policy think-tanks freely available on-line. As you read about a favourite political issue, make sure you read many perspectives so that you develop your critical eye and form your own opinions.

-Love to talk and socialize with friends? Form a discussion group or a book club. Encourage everyone to read the chosen book, podcast, or movie and prepare questions ahead of time to jumpstart your club's lively discussion.

-Did you love art as a child? Pick up a set of paints or pencils – they don't have to be expensive. Go on-line or borrow a book from the library on your favourite artist or style of art. Give it a whirl, don't aim for perfection, enjoy the challenge!

-Have you ever tried crossword puzzles? After just a few short weeks, you'll notice a significant change in your skills. A daily exercise for your mind will strengthen your brain. Plus, there is great evidence that daily workouts for your mind will help to keep you sharp as you age.

## Step 2: Set incremental milestones

As you begin each week, identify one small, obtainable, and measurable goal that you will work on over the course of the next 7 days. Slow and steady is the pace here: choose one achievable goal at the start of each week. Do not identify goals in advance for future weeks; take it one week at a time. Just like a baby learning to crawl, allow yourself to enjoy this exciting early phase of your journey. Resist the temptation to race to the finish line. Happiness comes from the pursuit of achieving your goals; and remember, there is no pot of gold at the finish line. Live in the present and be grateful for where you are currently in the journey toward your goal.

## Step 3: Gather your data

At the end of each week, reflect on your goal and the process of attempting or achieving success. Do not judge yourself. Approach this reflection as an impartial observer— like an objective researcher. Did you find success?

Were there situations in your life that distracted you from achieving success? If so, what were these distractions, and could they be avoided or reduced in the future? The point in charting our success is twofold: it will help you track the progress of the slow and steady pace of accomplishing your goals. And, importantly, it provides you with "teachable moments" that you can use to understand yourself; that inner voice that can sometimes be your friend and cheerleader, or, at times, your foe and critical naysayer. Get to know your inner voice. When we do not make a concerted effort to listen and recognize our inner voice, it doesn't mean it isn't affecting us. Quite the contrary.

Your inner voice is always talking to you, but until we condition ourselves to hear it, we are at risk of incorporating its messages without first filtering its potential negativity.

As you reflect on your efforts in pursuing your goal you are also conditioning yourself to recognize your inner voice, determining if it is friend or foe. If you soon discover that your inner voice is critical and negative, you can then begin the process of reconditioning it to become your friend and cheerleader. Tapping into your inner voice and recalibrating it to be your ally is the secret to creating happiness in your life.

Step 4: Celebrate your accomplishments

Have you ever punished yourself for bad behaviour? Maybe you 'cheated' on your diet, and as a consequence you severely limited your food intake the following day. It is almost a natural reaction: when we are disappointed by ourselves for our perceived lack of willpower or motivation, we react critically to ourselves. Our inner voice becomes foe, and we take punitive action toward ourselves with the intent to bolster our willpower for next time.

But this doesn't work, does it? In fact, quite the opposite. When we turn up the volume on our inner foe voice, we become our own worst enemy. And, chances are, our lack of perceived willpower diminishes even further. Such is the nature of relapse; it can often snowball from one small slip-up to the total abandonment of your goals.

So, if punishing yourself doesn't work, what does? Let's try something completely different. When reflecting on whether you attained your weekly goal, turn up the volume on your inner friend voice. Let this voice help you understand why you weren't able to successfully complete your weekly goal. Be gentle on yourself, find the silver-lining, and celebrate your commitment to the pursuit of personal growth. After all, the secret to happiness is not found in achieving your goals, but in discovering and working toward your goals.

Enjoy the process and remember the analogy of childhood: if your goal is to run, you must first learn to crawl, to toddle, to walk, and then to run. There is nothing wrong in learning to crawl first; in fact, it is completely necessary. Enjoy this experience and this phase of your journey toward success. You will eventually find success in running, but you will find happiness in the pursuit of your goals. Enjoy the moment, learn from your struggles, recognize your strengths, and celebrate your successes, no matter how small.

# CHAPTER 4

## Rule 4: Raise your village

*Develop a support system for optimal parenting*

In my professional roles over the past two and a half decades, I have dedicated my working life to the study of children's development and the advancement of progressive social policies and programs that benefit children and honour their inherent rights of citizenship. I am an academic scholar on the history of childhood and have written extensively about society's constructions of children and how these views and values impact women and their roles as mothers. I acknowledge this academic experience in order to lend credibility to the recommendations I make for rule 4: raise your village.

A few years back, I came across a video my daughter shared on her Instagram page. There was Maggie, on the couch at her friend Beth's house. It was family movie night at the Jefferson's and my daughter was cozied up, under a blanket, with a large bowl of popcorn on her lap and Beth's mom, Tessa, nestled beside her. Maggie and Tessa had their arms around each other, posed for the camera. My daughter tagged the video "my second mom".

I'm not going to lie; those two words pierced my heart like an arrow. After crying a few tears, I knew I needed to sort out my emotions and understand why I was reacting in this way. After some reflection, I realized I felt jealous of Tessa and Maggie's relationship; I was hurt that I was missing this lovely moment in my daughter's young life; I felt excluded; and you guessed it—I felt the shame of being a terrible mother. A mother so terrible, in fact, that my daughter required a second mother just to offset the terribleness of my poor mothering. My pride was wounded, plain and simple.

But as an academic scholar in children's development research, I knew, in my head, that my daughter's development was only enriched by her wide circle of supportive and nurturing friends, including her amazing and lovely second mom. There are countless examples, in cross-cultural studies far and wide, that demonstrate the advantages of "village parenting". It takes a village to raise a child, as the adage goes, and yet, our Western culture plays lip service to this sage advice. When it comes right down to it, we don't want a village to raise our children. We want to be everything and everyone—indeed, the only one—to our children. I even know a woman who feels threatened by her own husband when he takes on too much of the nurturer role with their children.

Ask any mother, and she will deftly tell you about the theory of childhood attachment. Our children, they will incant, must form healthy positive attachments in their early years in order to form healthy positive attachments in their older years. I don't dispute the basic premise of attachment, but, as a children's development expert, let me tell you the Untold Truth behind this patriarchal-fueled theory.

After World War II, male soldiers returned from war and began to re-enter the labour market. This presented a bit of a problem for the many women who had filled the shoes of men in these various job roles. Alongside the return of men to the workforce, and the forthcoming displacement of women from these jobs, came, conveniently, a theory of children's attachment that would send women and mothers racing back to their domestic roles. John Bowlby's attachment theory emphasized the importance of early attachment, though, somewhere along the way, his ideas on parent-child attachment became tainted by monotropism. In this context, monotropism is the belief that babies and young children can only form healthy positive attachment styles through the primary relationship with a sole caregiver, the mother. Influenced by this viewpoint, women were socially pressured to abandon their positions in the labour market and turn their jobs over to the returning men soldiers. As such, monotropism became widely accepted as the best way to parent a child.

But the Untold Truth of the matter is, there are many ways for babies and young children to form attachments in their early years. A look to cross-cultural and historical studies proves just that. The Western notion of monotropism is not the universal norm, it just happens to be North America's norm of the past few decades. Other cultures embrace many different ways to nurture babies to form healthy positive attachments, ways that include multiple caregivers—including fathers and extended family caregivers. Indeed, in pre-colonization, members of North America's Cree First Nation raised their children by many mothers; children would call several women by the name "mother". In other non-Western cultures, it can be the father or an extended family member who takes on the primary caregiver role.

I'm not suggesting any one approach to parenting is better than the other; rather, I'm holding up evidence that women have long been duped into believing that the monotropism way of parenting is the only way to parent. It's not. It's just Western society's current norm. Once you understand this cultural context, you can't help but realize that the pressure you have experienced from the impossible standard of monotropism, coupled with the struggle to succeed in your career, is completely and utterly man-made.

So, back to my daughter's second mom. Even though I was fully aware of the monotropism myth, I still fell for it. I was heartsick to know that my daughter had formed a meaningful attachment to a second mother figure. I was not immune to the cultural myth of monotropism despite having the knowledge of this man-made falsehood. I had to dig deep. I had to fight the mom guilt. I began to write about my feelings in a journal. And as I did, I was reminded of how fortunate I was that my daughter had a second mom. As a busy working mom, I desperately needed the support of a parenting village—I still do, even with my daughter now fully grown. And so do most women, especially working mothers. Why then, I asked myself, do we play lip service to the idea of "it takes a village to raise a child"?

Indeed, while we may recite the village parenting adage to others, many of us have no intention of applying it in our own lives. Sure, it might be fine for some moms to rely on a village of support, but not those of us winning the mom race: the perfect moms. And, so, we become the architects of our own nightmare. We inflate our sense of self-importance, we downplay the parenting skills of our children's fathers—though different than our own style, surely, but important fatherly instincts nonetheless—and we reject the help and support of our village. Until, desperate for help, we find ourselves in over our heads, at a breaking point. It's a prison of our own making, but it's not our fault. We are the product of our Western culture.

But now that you know the Untold Truth behind attachment theory, it's time to embrace your village. Your village may come in many forms: your child's father (whether you are romantically partnered with him or not), your mother, mother-in-law, or, as in the majority of cases, your childcare provider. So many women are surrounded by a veritable village, yet, because of mom guilt, they refuse to take the extended hand offered. I say: embrace your village. Be thankful you have the support of loved ones and friendships, and, when it is your turn to "be the village" to another mom— and it will be—be grateful for the opportunity to give back and lighten her load.

A few months back, I read a quote by celebrity mom, the new mom-hero for today's generation of young mothers. In doling out her advice she explained how she fights a particular impulse with her children whenever they complain of her absence when she leaves for work obligations. Rather than explain to them that she must leave them so she can earn a living, she said she fights this instinct. She does not want to burden her children with any guilt that might arise should they become aware of her need to earn money.

Instead, she apologizes for her absence and promises them that she will make up for the missed time. She further advised to never admonish your children about how your career affords them their lifestyle. I think her message is loud and clear—and woefully misguided. I believe she is telling other working moms that while it may be challenging to juggle it all, never let your kids know about the hard reality of being a parent—paying the mortgage, financing the private tutor, affording the holidays. But why can't our children know about the realities of having to earn a living? This celebrity mom's so-called advice is really damaging, and it's rooted in the monotropism myth.

Remember, the monotropism myth is a vestige of the World War II-era plot to keep women away from the jobs and career choices that men desire. You are not causing your child irreversible damage by employing a childcare provider. Nor will your child stop loving you should you leave her in the care of her father, a grandparent, or an older sibling. I won't get into the mountains of research that prove the positive impacts of high-quality childcare (but I could; it exists), but I will flag one bit of evidence for your attention: should you come across a study on the harms of out-of-home childcare on children's development, use a critical eye to examine its methodology—these studies are most surely flawed. In many cases, they don't consider quality of care as an influencing variable. Or you can just trust me on this one. I wrote my PhD dissertation on early childhood learning and I can tell you with confidence that high-quality childcare provides enriching and enhancing early childhood experiences for all children, which benefits their development.

Of course, I hope it goes without saying that I am not suggesting you never see your kids. But I want to also point out a body of knowledge that tells us that today's working mothers—despite their 9-to-5 work obligations—are spending more quantity time with their children than any generation of mothers before them. Yep, you heard me right. Not only are women working out of the home for a good chunk of the work week; we are also spending more time parenting our children than the generation of mothers before us. How is this possible, you might ask? Well, let's think about it through the lens of our own childhoods. I will use my own experience as a child growing up in the 1970s. In my younger years, for the most part, my mom was a stay-at-home mother. She was there at lunchtime, welcoming my sister and me home over the noon hour with a nice hot bowl of soup and a made-to-order sandwich. She was there after school, with a healthy and nutritious before-dinner snack. She deftly put supper on the table, and then whisked away the dirty dinner plates. She organized bath time, she made sure homework was done, and she tucked us into bed at the end of a long day. Sound familiar? I bet you, too, are ensuring breakfasts, lunches and dinners are prepared and eaten. I bet you, too, are shepherding the homework and bath time and bedtime routines of your little one. But unlike the motherhood expectations of the 1970s, I bet you are also down on the floor with your children, facilitating endless educational play opportunities, and zipping from one organized sport event or dance rehearsal or artistic class to the next, all the while, figuring out how to squeeze in your paid work obligations in the process.

It's true: despite the balancing act of paid employment and parenting, most of today's working mothers are spending more quality time and quantity time with our children than the prior generation of full-time moms. And, while you are away from your children, earning a living, your village, whether it be your child's father, a family member, or loving early childhood educator, is providing wonderful care and early learning opportunities for your child during your absence. There is no need to feel guilty about it. So, let's banish working mom guilt once and for all. Indeed, let us close the chapter on it!

CHAPTER 5


**Rule 5: Mind your gut**

*Treat food as medicine and eat for your mental health*


I am not going to fill the pages of this chapter with myriad diet suggestions. Nor am I going to presume that we all share the same resources, cultural backgrounds, and culinary skills that lend themselves to one diet or the next. And I'm also not going to assume we are all trying to maintain a trim waistline. Healthy bodies come in many different shapes and sizes; I abhor the gendered notion of 'the perfect body' and the punishing food restrictions that come with it. Far too many women place their self-worth on their jean size and engage in self-harmful thinking about their post-baby bodies. With all this in mind, I have just one rule about diet: eat for your mental health.

Emphasizing your mental wellbeing over fluctuating numbers on a scale will lead you toward healthier nutrition habits, the goals of which are consistency and sustainability. I have found that by focusing my family's nutritional needs through the lens of positive mental health, I am less focused on trendy diets and restrictive eating. I am also well aware that, for better or worse, I am a role model for my daughter. Since Maggie was little, I have known my attitudes and actions related to nutrition and body image impact my daughter. Early on, I vowed to myself that my daughter would never hear me speak self-critically about my body or its various parts; nor would she see me starving myself to drop a few pounds. Any positive feedback I have given my daughter about her body, throughout her childhood, has always focused on her athleticism, her strength, and her health.

As a working mother, I am proud to have raised a daughter, now a young woman, who has a positive body image. Notwithstanding the ups and downs of womanhood, the always-present male gaze that sexualizes young women (and, sadly, girls), and the curated photo-shopped images of 'real' beauty across social media platforms, my daughter is, for the most part, strong and healthy. Of course, I am not a 19-year-old woman, and I cannot possibly imagine the pressures young women face to look Instagram-ready and effortlessly thin. But I do know that shifting the focus away from the body and emphasizing nutrition as a way to bolster her mental health helped to offset the potential damage of society's body-obsessed culture in her adolescent years.

I also know that embracing nutrition and the power of food as a way to improve our mental health is an approach that sits comfortably with my husband. In this way, rule 5: mind your gut is an easy-ish sell for men; perhaps more so than, say, counseling or pharmacology—at least in my family home. But if eating for your mental health is not an easy sell in your family home, try this: keep it a secret. If you sense family opposition to "food as medicine", make small incremental changes to your family's nutritional habits. Start by eliminating foods that disrupt the body's microbiome, and replace them with sneaky substitutes (cauliflower rice, gluten-free flour, sugar-free treats). Your family may not be on board with these substitutes, but if done right, they'll never even know—and yet they will still reap the benefits of a happier, healthier gut.

A lot of attention is paid to our brains—we consider it the driver of the bus, so to speak. But less attention has been paid to the important role of the gut in our health and mental health. This is starting to change, however; expert scientists now view the gut as our "second brain" and are finally giving this bodily system the credit it's due.

The gut includes our stomach, liver, kidneys, small intestine, large intestine, and, importantly, our microbiome. The microbiome—our gut bacteria or gut flora—is no small matter; if added up, altogether it would weigh between 3 and 5 pounds, about as much as our brain.

Our gut has a very important role in our health. Remember the autonomic nervous system reviewed in rule 1: outfox family stress? Well, it is not just our brain that activates our fight-or-flight responses to stress; our gut does this as well. When you think about it, this makes sense. If you were to eat something poisonous, you need an alert-system that springs into action to expel the toxic you injected. Think of the microbiome as millions of tiny soldiers, working together and sending messages back and forth to your brain to keep your body healthy and happy.

The gut and the brain are connected via the vagus nerve, a two-way communication system that enables the brain to talk to the gut, and the gut to talk to the brain. Through strong two-way communication, a healthy microbiome improves brain functioning and supports positive mental health. And a healthy microbiome tells the brain that we are safe and free from threat. In contrast, an unhealthy microbiome sends stress signals to the brain, resulting in a negative feedback loop that compromises our health and our mental wellness. So, how do we achieve a healthy microbiome? Well, like so many things, it comes back to a wise old adage: we are what we eat (and drink).

A healthy microbiome is nurtured through a diverse diet—we want a microbiome comprised of vast and varied gut bacteria. A narrowly constricted diet begets a narrowly constricted microbiome.

As I've said, I'm not going to promote any one type of diet. The dietary choices you make for your family must be made in consideration of your culture, your family income, your geography, and your time. But what I will say is aim for real food; the biggest threat to a healthy microbiome is a diet overrun with heavily processed foods. Build your family's nutrition around a variety of plants and vegetables—in season and garden fresh, whenever possible. I, myself, am no green thumb, but I manage to grow a few pots of tomatoes and lettuce each summer season. But if a small vegetable garden is not feasible for you, you might be able to find a neighbourhood urban farmer who sells fresh grown produce.

The next step in this Zen House Rule is to apply your field researcher role in observing your family's diet and their food reactions. Keep a meal journal and start making connections between what you and your loved ones eat and how you and your loved ones feel.

Remember, you are eating for your mental health. Look for changes—good or bad—in how your family's mood responds to new foods or certain diets. In my own family home, I have discovered that gluten and sugar disrupt our sense of harmony and balance. My husband and I have also discovered that alcohol does not mix well with his PTSD. To this end, he has eliminated alcohol from his diet and lifestyle. Now, rather than a cold beer or a glass of wine with friends, Tony enjoys a bit of recreational cannabis instead. And after seeing improvements in his mental health after making this switch, I've followed suit. While I haven't completely banished alcohol from my lifestyle, I know I feel better when I keep my intake in check. Experimenting with different cannabis strains with my husband has been fun, much like discovering a new grape in the world of wine. Of course, we practice caution, always making sure to stick with lower THC strains. In my family home, there is no stigma surrounding cannabis. If you are a guest of legal age in my house, you'll be offered red, white, or green.

The other important part of rule 5: mind your gut is to ensure you share the responsibility for meal preparation, cooking, and cleaning-up among all your family members, even (especially!) your kids. As the mom of the house, you may be the chef of your kitchen—the planner of the meal, the procurer of ingredients—but you needn't be sous chef, pastry chef, and dishwasher as well. Share the workload and make dinner time a collaborative affair.

If you find that you don't have time to make home-cooked meals, consider ready-to-make meal plans, rather than picking up the take-out menu of your local pizza place or opening that bag of hotdogs—remember, you want to nurture a healthy microbiome, which comes from real food, not processed food. And you never know, there may be a local meal service in your neighbourhood that makes ready-for-the-oven meals that you can purchase on the cheap—even if it's just once a week to provide you with a nice break.

The last suggestion I will make is to remember that meals are just sustenance. Somewhere along the way, in Western culture, cooking for your family has become conflated with the status symbol of the perfect wife/perfect mom facade. Hot breakfasts during the work week and stylized Bento box lunches for school have somehow become the norm working mothers are expected to achieve. But just like the monotropism myth we reviewed in rule 4: raise your village, this, too, is rooted in patriarchy. Equating the perfect family meal with the perfect family life is a gendered falsehood meant to impose guilt on the working mother. Do not fall for it. The main purpose of food is to provide sustenance. Sure, if and when you have the time, meals can take on more importance (first day of school breakfast, special birthday dinners). But when you don't have the time (or skills or interest or budget) your goal should be simple: assemble a nutritious meal, with the help of your family members, that grows a healthy microbiome.

The other myth surrounding family mealtime comes from the notion that families who share dinner together are the happiest families. This nonsense reeks of a traditional view of motherhood—it is, again, that gendered notion that should a woman work outside her home, she must compensate by ensuring perfect meals for her family. Remember, food is just sustenance; mealtime should not be an assessment of your family's bond and the quality of your mothering. There are many different ways family members bond with one another. Walking the dog together after work and school. Practicing mindful living and positive self-talk together. Doing yoga together in the living room. Having a dance party in the kitchen. It is not a three-course gourmet meal that bonds a family. It is the act of coming together, whatever the format, that nurtures a healthier, happier family home. Good nutrition is the main goal of any meal, plain and simple. An apple and a cheese slice are excellent car-friendly breakfasts for you and your loved ones. And a slapped-together nutritious dinner, compliments of your neighbourhood ready-to-warm meal program, is just perfect enough.

CHAPTER 6

**Rule 6: Count your sleep**

*Harness the power of sleep to protect your family's wellness*

The cruel irony of sleep is the more you need it, the harder it is to get. Do you find yourself dragging your sleep-deprived bones out of bed in the mornings, only to lie in bed the next night, tossing and turning? Do you get less than seven hours of restful sleep each day? If this sounds like you or your loved ones, chances are this lack of sleep has taken a toll on your health. What researchers now know about the science of sleep has grown tremendously in the past decade. While there is still much yet to understand, many experts agree that sleep is the foundation to a healthier, happier life.

Sleep nurtures and restores our body, including, importantly, our brain. In essence, a good night's sleep enhances your ability to learn, to perform, and to regulate emotion. It improves your immune system (if you sleep less than seven hours per night, you are three more times likely to catch a cold). Poor sleep, on the other hand, compromises your health and mental health, makes you prone to illness, increases your risk of cancer, and can even lead to weight gain. And yet, for those who suffer from poor sleep, many accept their affliction as just part of life's fate. But if there is just one consideration you take from reading this chapter, let it be this: if you suffer from a lack of sleep, treat this malady as you would any other illness; tell your healthcare professional and work together to find a solution.

In my family home, I value sleep as one of the most powerful tools of wellness I have in my toolbox. It is the basis of my health and mental health, and that of my loved ones.

But this wasn't always my attitude. When my daughter was a young teenager, it used to drive me crazy to see her sleep in on weekends or during holidays. And when my husband was working shift work on the fire department, it used to irritate me to find him napping on his afternoons off. I am not a napper, and I saw Tony's afternoon sleeping routine as a big waste of time. For myself, I was prone to viewing sleep as an indulgence—something I needed, yes, but something that could be put on the back burner if competing demands took precedence. Looking back at the misconceptions I held about sleep—that my teenager was being lazy, that my husband was wasting precious family time, that sleep was secondary in my list of priorities—I am disappointed in myself. But I didn't know then what I do know now.

Sleep is our body's greatest defense mechanism. It regulates our metabolic state by balancing our insulin and glucose levels.

It nurtures a healthy gut and microbiome and regulates our appetite. And it helps us regulate our moods and our emotions. It is, quite simply, a one-stop shop for health and wellness.

Our brains are hard-wired with an internal 24-hour clock that creates our individual circadian rhythm. This clock is called the suprachiasmatic nucleus. Each of us has a unique circadian rhythm, but for the most part we fall into two types: morning birds or night owls; though, some of us are a mix of both. Our bodies signal sleep when our brain's clock releases melatonin. That is why melatonin supplements are used by some people to help them fall asleep (but they don't help us stay asleep; they are not a sedative).

To better understand the power of sleep, it is important to understand the process of sleep. There are different cycles and types of sleep.

Each cycle of sleep lasts approximately ninety minutes (one and a half hours). The optimal duration of sleep per night is five cycles, which yields approximately eight hours of sleep. Within each cycle of sleep are five stages of sleep: four stages of non-rapid eye movement (NREM) sleep, followed by the last and fifth stage of rapid eye movement (REM) sleep.

Sleep scientists believe that during NREM sleep the brain organizes and makes sense of our new memories. In REM sleep, which comes after four phases of NREM sleep, the brain integrates these new memories within our existing memory bank. Both types of sleep are important, and one cannot happen without the other.

While much is still unknown, REM sleep is associated with fast brain waves. Our brains are extremely active in REM sleep, as active as when we are engaged in deep thinking and concentration when we are awake.

Once a sleep cycle is complete, the process begins all over again as we enter the next sleep cycle. We move through the four stages of NREM sleep, followed by the fifth stage of REM sleep. In an ideal sleep scenario, this pattern repeats for five cycles of sleep. Importantly, it is in the last two cycles of sleep when you get the most REM sleep. In other words, the last three hours of your sleep (the early morning hours) is when you get the most benefit from REM sleep.

If you're doing the math, this means that to reap the full benefits of sleep you need to sleep through five 90-minute cycles of sleep, which is approximately eight hours. When you sleep less than this amount of time, you fail to get that important REM sleep that occurs in the final three hours of a good night's rest. And if you are convinced that you are a person who needs less than seven or eight hours of sleep each night, the odds are against this.

There is a very small proportion of people in the world that can function well on less than seven or eight hours of sleep. This is due to their genetic mutation—the short sleep gene—which occurs in less than 3% of the population. Most of us—the other 97%—need (not want, not prefer, but need) between seven and nine hours of sleep. When we fail to get this optimal amount, we don't just lose an hour or two of rest, we lose much of that precious REM sleep, the "medicinal ingredient" of a good night's sleep. You can try to cheat the system that is our biology, but the result is much like running your car on gas fumes—you will sputter and eventually stall. Just as a high-performance car needs a full tank of gas, a well-functioning you needs your sleep.

Teenagers have different circadian rhythms than adults. While it may seem that their tendency to stay up all night and sleep all day is meant to annoy us, it truly is a by-product of their unique brain clocks. Their suprachiasmatic nucleus dictates their late to bed, late to rise lifestyle.

The melatonin that signals sleepiness in your teenager is released far later in the evening than yours. Denying a teenager their preferred sleep schedule is simply misplaced maternal care. Of course, societal rules and norms often dictate the sleep schedule of your child, but wherever possible, take into consideration the preferred sleeping habits of a teenager. If there is flexibility in choosing a class schedule for school, encourage your child to select for a late-morning start time. If there is flexibility in training options for your teenager's sport, encourage the coach to opt for evening practices rather than early morning ones. And on weekends and holidays, let your sleeping teenager sleep.

Re-framing your teenager's sleep habits as simply the biomechanics of the teenage brain may help you to see their refusal to conform to your early to bed-early to rise sleep schedule in a new light.

I found this to be the case in my own family home. I used to see my daughter's sleeping habits as indulgent and lazy—and a wasting of time, the biggest sin of all in my books. But after learning more about the science of sleep, I began reexamining my old views of sleeping.

When my daughter was a baby, I protected her sleep like a sentinel on guard. I did everything in my power to keep her sleep routine consistent and reliable; to keep the surrounding noise low and the interruptions to a minimum. I knew she was happier on a regular sleep schedule, and I certainly was happier when she was happier. So why didn't I apply this same protective mothering instinct to my teenaged daughter?

Again, engrained values about sleep as an indulgence were to blame. I had to learn a new attitude toward sleep, and that meant unlearning my misinformed thinking.

After researching the power of sleep, I began to see sleep as the opposite of wasting time. I realized that sleep was not inactive or passive, it was active—indeed, our brains are hard at work while we sleep. Sleep research shows that our brain waves are extremely fast during the sleep cycle, especially during REM sleep. While it may look like we are doing nothing while we sleep, we are, in fact, engaged in one of the best wellness strategies we have at our disposal. If you are a mom to a teenager who loves to sleep in, remember that they are engaged in a wellness activity. By sleeping, they are nurturing their health and wellness. In today's world, we worry about the mental health of our teenagers. We focus on their screen time and their exposure to social media.

But insufficient sleep should be our biggest worry—a lack of sleep for children, especially teenagers, is linked to drug and alcohol problems, anxiety, and attention disorders.

The point in describing these risks is not to add to your worries as a mother, but to help you understand how important it is to protect the sleep of your children. Just as you would monitor their screen time, you should, too, safeguard their sleep. And just as you would never wake a sleeping baby, you should never wake a sleeping teenager.

The shift work schedule of my husband, when he was a first responder, took a serious toll on his ability to get a good night's sleep. And, while I know the vicarious trauma he was exposed to was certainly the trigger to his PTSD, I also believe his ability to recover from this trauma was complicated by his chaotic and disruptive sleep schedule.

Sleep research shows that when people are sleep deprived, they are much more likely to have emotional regulation difficulties and their fight or flight responses are easily triggered.

If you find yourself feeling moody, or you and your partner are struggling to get along, the problem might just be a lack of sleep. Try getting to bed earlier so you can get those five cycles of sleep each night.

There are many tips and tricks for establishing good sleep hygiene and healthy sleep routines. Depending on your unique circadian rhythm, you will need to determine for yourself the best sleep routine for you. I am an early bird and I function best on nine hours of sleep. I am also very fortunate to be a good sleeper; I can fall asleep quickly, and I tend to stay asleep throughout the night. I typically go to bed at 10:00PM and wake up at 7:00AM. I have tried other sleep schedules, but this is the best pattern for me. I don't follow it with absolute rigidity—I will stay up late for summer parties and concerts—but for most of my nights, this is my routine.

My husband, on the other hand, is a biphasic sleeper. Whether this is a trait of his Greek heritage, or a by-product of his first responder days, Tony sleeps six to seven hours a night, with a one-and-a-half-hour nap during the day. I used to judge his daily napping habit; I thought it was ruining his nighttime sleep routine. But as a biphasic sleeper, Tony's natural sleep routine is divided into two: his nighttime sleep and his daytime sleep, together of which give him eight to nine hours of sleep.

To determine your body's circadian rhythm and that of your loved ones, reach for your notebook and put on your field researcher's hat. Track your own sleeping habits to determine what precedes a good night's sleep and what interferes with it. Some people are extremely sensitive to caffeine, and while they may limit their coffee or tea intake by noon, they may not be aware of the caffeine found in their evening chocolate ritual. Alcohol before bed can also interfere with sleep.

If you have grown accustomed to enjoying a glass of wine in the evening, try having your wine with dinner instead. Or you might consider eliminating alcohol altogether, opting instead for a small dose of evening cannabis. I know of many women who have found great success in using cannabis edibles as a sleep aid. Cannabis in edible form is metabolized slower compared to smoke or vape; this means its effects last longer, approximately eight hours, the length of time of an ideal sleep. If you are new to cannabis, do some research to find the best strain for yourself. Don't be afraid to head to your local cannabis store and talk to one of their experts. For most of the women I know who have found cannabis to be an effective sleep aid, they lean toward indica strains which tend to bring on calmness and sleepiness (sativa strains, on the other hand, are your best bet for a fun night out with your gal pals!).

Most people cannot easily transition from activity to sleep. To this end, a regular nighttime routine that gently transitions your brain and body into sleep readiness is extremely powerful. Consistency is key, especially when you are first establishing a healthy sleep routine. If your goal is to go to bed by 10:00PM, you should begin your sleep transition at 9:00PM. A warm bath or shower is shown to be helpful, not because the warm water heats our bodies, but, conversely, because it cools our bodies. After a warm bath, the exposure to the cooler air temperature cools our bodies down, and a cooler body temperature is very helpful for sleep. You might also wish to try turning your thermostat down a couple of degrees in the evenings. A programmable thermostat is perfect for this.

Another important strategy for transitioning into sleep readiness is eliminating or limiting screen time an hour before bed. If you haven't already done so, try programming your smart phone to its nighttime setting in the early evening. This decreases the blue light emission of your smart phone, which is the enemy of sleep. Consider, also, the lightbulbs in your main living areas. You may wish to try lower watt bulbs, as bright light exposure can keep sleepiness at bay.

Are you exercising too late in the day? If you are having trouble falling asleep, consider moving your workout to the mornings instead of after work. You might also try getting more sunlight during the day; consistent exposure to morning sunlight is especially good for recalibrating our circadian rhythms.

The last strategy I will recommend is the most powerful one, especially for women who are prone to worry—those of us who cannot seem to turn off our brains. While trying to fall asleep, many of us will ruminate over the items on our To-Do lists that did not get done, or we fret about the next day's busy schedule. If this sounds like you, I encourage you to revisit rule 2: upgrade your brain. A consistent practice of bedtime meditation can be very effective in helping you to silence the onslaught of worried thoughts. And this practice need not be lengthy—try a ten-minute session each evening and see if you can commit to this routine for a minimum of four weeks. Make it your goal for personal growth and follow the steps I outlined in rule 4: play for life. Informed by the science of motivation, these steps are effective at sustaining healthy habits for optimal sleep hygiene.

Before I end this chapter, let me ask you this: what would you do if you woke up in the morning with a bleeding nose? If this occurred once, you may likely ignore it.

But if you kept waking up with a bleeding nose for weeks or months on end, I suspect you would seek out professional help from your healthcare provider. Now let me ask you this: do you wake up most mornings exhausted after a restless night's sleep? Are you unable to get at least seven hours of sleep most nights? And have you suffered from this condition for weeks, months, even years on end? If you are unable to get the sleep you need, treat this symptom like you would that bleeding nose—do not ignore it and chalk it up to "that's just how I am".  Just as you would take yourself to see your physician if you were having a health problem, take yourself to your healthcare professional if you are consistently having trouble sleeping.  Waking up exhausted each morning after a fitful night of insomnia is a warning sign—one you should take seriously. Protect your sleep and the sleep of your loved ones; and make sure to get at least seven hours of it— this dose of sleep is as fundamental to your health as oxygen, water, and food.

# CHAPTER 7

**Rule 7: Lean back (not in)**

*Apply the science of recovery and banish motherhood guilt*

Self-compassion is the foundation to rule 7: lean back (not in). Self-compassion comes from being, not doing. And it comes from leaning back, not in (sorry, Sheryl Sandberg). If this sounds too easy, or overly simplified, it's not. If it sounds unattainable, or utterly non-sensical, it's not that either.

What is the key to nurturing a healthier happier home for your family? In a word: you. As a woman, a wife, and a mother, you take care of your family. From bribing your little one to eat her vegetables, to coaxing your teenager away from his screens, to monitoring the cholesterol levels of your husband, you wage the never-ending battle to ensure a healthy lifestyle for your loved ones. The responsibility looms heavy. Add in the hectic schedule of full-time work, and it's no wonder the willpower to maintain our own healthy lifestyle is zapped by the end of a long day. We think: how could we possibly live without our nightly glass (or three) of pinot? And yet, despite our exhaustion, we lie awake at night, desperate to fall asleep, but unable to power down our worried minds.

To some extent, we accept our suffering health as the new normal of today. But this need not be the case. We do not have to sacrifice our health and happiness as the plight of today's working mother. The high-quality of life that good health affords must be our standard; the era of forsaking our wellness in the interest of doing more, being more, or giving more for our children and our spouses is over.

I have heard a version of this story from countless women: once my kids are older, I'll finally have time to exercise. Or: my kids will only be young once, so I don't mind sacrificing this time in my life to give them everything they want.

As a research translator with a specialization in the sociology of childhood, I know well the evolution of society's cultural values toward children. Never before in history has society romanticized the notion of the perfect childhood as we do now. Today's society treats its children as its most precious resource. But could it be the pendulum has swung just a bit too far?

At no other time in history have mothers spent so much of their personal time on parenting. This may surprise you. It surprised me, too. We working moms know well the heart-piercing guilt of stretching our time to meet the competing priorities of home and work. Yet, despite the demands on the working mother, we spend more quantity time with our children than any other time in history.

Imagine your own childhoods. You may have had a working mother yourself, but chances are her schedule was far less demanding than your own.

If you are like most us from this bygone era, your mother was not in the stands rooting for you at your every practice or game. Nor was she on call, car keys in hand, ready to transport you from one social event to the next. With this comparison in mind, the research rings true, doesn't it? Mothers of today spend more time with their children than ever before, despite the added workload of paid employment. And, given time is finite, the only way today's working mother can possibly squeeze in the work-home demands on her day is to squeeze herself out.

Sound familiar?

The guilt of the working mother is one of the greatest barriers to our health. Recognizing and reconciling this guilt is critical to your journey toward wellness.

Your health and happiness are just as important as that of your loved ones. Indeed, your wellness sets the standard in your family home. If you want health and happiness for your own children, you must first begin with yourself. Banish any lingering working mom guilt you may have and take comfort in the fact that you are leading by example the kind of parent you want your child to become. Make no mistake, your health and happiness are equally as important as the health and happiness of those you love. Just as the airline steward tells you to put your oxygen mask on first before rescuing your loved ones, you must first look after your own health before nurturing the health of your loved ones.

I'm going to be honest, leaning back is hard to do, especially for those of us who suffer from the perfect wife/perfect mother complex. If this sounds like you, think of leaning back as the important act of recovery. Recovery is a concept well known in the world of athletics and sports. High achieving athletes credit their recovery days (or rest days) as essential to improving their performance. They understand that recovery is the foundation to growth. After an intense workout or performance, a rest day or two provides the necessary recovery time for the body to heal, adapt, and grow in its capacity for peak performance. The term self-care reflects this concept of recovery. But be careful. If you are an over-achiever type, you may find yourself stressed out over the need to schedule self-care into your busy day—which defeats the point of recovery. Recovery should be the act of removing stress from your day, not adding it.

If this rule proves difficult for you, try to remember that by practicing recovery you are modeling positive self-care for your children. And isn't that the whole point of mothering, after all? We want to raise our children to take care of their own health and happiness. We want them to practice self-love and self-compassion; we don't want them to sacrifice themselves for their own children or their own careers once they grow up. Recovery, or leaning back, is an important way to model positive self-compassion for your loved ones, and this should help you banish any lingering guilt in taking time for yourself. In my personal practice of recovery, this is what I know:

- Recovery is not a hobby. A hobby can be put off for when we have the time. I don't squeeze in my recovery routine into my busy day, it is the cornerstone to my day. I don't feel guilty about practicing recovery; instead, I feel compassion for the too busy working mothers who don't/can't/won't model positive self-care for their children.

- Leaning back doesn't mean we don't care—of course we care! As women, that is our defining quality. Rather, it means that we shift ourselves away from the pursuit of external validation toward that of internal validation. We replace self-esteem—which comes from perfecting our lives and our homes and ticking off the growing number of items on our To-Do list—with self-compassion, which comes from the unconditional love of self. Once we make this shift, the voice in our head becomes softer, kinder, and more maternal. We mother ourselves, you could say. The tender gentle voice we use to sooth the tummy ache or the tears of our children, we apply to ourselves. We become worthy of such tenderness, not because we are accomplished career women, or self-sacrificing mothers-of-the-year, or yummy mummies who've maintained our trim waistlines, but because we are, quite simply, worthy of such love. Let me illustrate with my own story.

Like most women, I juggle the constant and competing demands of family and career. But with my daughter now grown, I have the wisdom of hindsight—I can see how I over-invested and over-worried as a mom when my daughter was younger. And I can also see how I lost myself in my attempt to support my husband in his recovery from PTSD. While not genetically related, Maggie and Tony are very alike—they are prone to episodes of anxiety, and, because I am their safety net, I often bear the brunt of their emotions. For years, it seemed that despite my best efforts to fortify myself and my personal mental health, I was always at the mercy of their moods. If my daughter was anxious about school or a quarrel with a friend, I became anxious too. If my husband was angry about politics or stressed out about finances, I took on his anger and stress too.

One day, after a particularly challenging time with my husband, I went for a bike ride. I love riding my bike in my sleepy lakeside village, and it always helps me refocus on the positives in my life. I let my mind wander, as I usually do, but on this particular bike ride I asked myself: why does my husband's mood dictate my own mood? With that simple question, everything became clear to me. I am in charge of my mood, not Tony. And no one, not even my loved ones, could take that power away from me. Right then and there, I made a commitment to myself. I decided I wanted to live a peaceful and joyful life. I decided I wanted to be a "glass half-full" type person. I decided I wanted to discuss family problems calmly—instead of arguing angrily. I decided I wanted to prioritize my physical and mental health through a commitment to regular exercise, outdoor activity, and a daily practice of mindfulness meditation. In essence, I committed to a new way of living.

Now I am in charge of my mood. I set out an intentional way to live each day through an early morning mantra. I support my husband and daughter in all the ways I can, but I don't own their moods or decisions. I prioritize my physical and mental health; it is not selfish to honour my commitment to daily self-care. I schedule my recovery time and I let my family know of my plans. I protect this time and my loved ones now know that my recovery time should not be interrupted unless it is an emergency (believe me, this was a learning process for them!).

In essence, I allow myself to put myself first, above my loved ones, for at least one hour each day. My family may try to guilt me into abandoning my planned recovery time, but I try to remember that by putting myself above them for this valuable (and short) time, I am modeling to them positive self-care so that they, too, will practice recovery. I do not want my daughter to be a martyr when she grows up and has kids of her own one day. I do not want to inadvertently model for her the harmful perfect wife/perfect mother complex. It is perfectly ok to be imperfect, and it is, in fact, good mothering to model self-care.

To be sure, I have let go of the perfect wife/perfect mother facade. I don't post 'Fakebook' photos on Facebook, I refuse to contribute to this charade. Instead, I ask for help when I need it. I don't allow myself to feel the pressure to handle every parenting task on my own. I delegate household chores—and I don't micromanage the way my husband and my daughter do them. I work smarter, not longer.

I am, however, meticulous at organizing my day so that I have dedicated time to do my "brain work" during the hours of the day when I'm most productive (mornings and early afternoons). I honour my work commitments, but I don't feel the need to outperform everyone else. I have let go of my overachiever ways. I show up, I work hard, and then I clock out. If I need to respond to evening emails, I make a point of shutting off my phone at a certain time in order to give myself a proper rest. And I no longer take my smart phone into the washroom with me (embarrassing, but true, I used to do this!). But, getting to this place was a process, believe me.

Learning how to lean back was born from a particularly hard week of balancing work life, PhD dissertation revisions, and parenting obligations. It seemed I could not get ahead. As I looked around, hoping my husband would read my mind and take care of dinner one night, I began to laugh at myself. I realized I had no one to blame for my exhaustion but myself. I kept taking on more and more tasks to juggle, and never once said "no" to anyone's requests. On the verge of an emotional breakdown, I realized I had to start putting myself first once in a while. And, being a researcher, I decided to approach this practice as a social experiment. I called it the Me First Every Once in a While experiment (herein, Me First).

The Me First experiment is the act of putting yourself first from time to time. At first, when I described the Me First experiment to my friends, they would laugh at my gumption. They wanted to know how my husband and daughter reacted (honestly, they barely even noticed). My gal pals wanted continuous play-by-play updates. My Me First experiment represented to them an outlandish act of rebellion. But in actuality, my experiment was just the simple act of saying no to my daughter and my husband every now and then. "No, Maggie", I would say, "you cannot use my computer to finish your school presentation until after I met an important work deadline—use a notepad and transcribe your work once I'm done". Or, "no, Maggie, I cannot pick you up from the mall, I am at my monthly book club meeting. You will have to take the bus home". Or it would be my husband's slow realization that there was nothing prepared for supper because I had made plans to go out for dinner with workmates on a night when Maggie was with her biological dad.

And here's what happened: my daughter became bus-savvy and grew more independent and responsible; and my husband became our household's best melted cheese sandwich-maker, a role he still relishes. I had expected a revolt by my acts of no, but to my surprise I discovered the positive benefits they held for my family. My husband and daughter had more father-daughter time; they made dinner together and discovered a mutual love of Scooby-doo re-runs. And I got to take a much-needed break from my family, reconnect with gal pals for dinner or book club or wine night, and return home happier and nurtured by my friendships (otherwise known as social buffering, a proven wellness strategy for enhancing longevity).

As I began sharing my Me First experiment, my friends and co-workers began their own Me First experiments. One colleague, Cindy, told me about an annual birthday party she threw for her husband and adult daughter who share a December 31st birthday. For the last fifteen years, this annual party grew in importance, expenditure, and time commitment. Slowly, the one-night party grew into a full weekend, with friends and family coming from far and wide. My friend Cindy had to plan and host not just one birthday party, but several breakfasts, lunches, outings, and activities.

After telling Cindy about my Me First experiment, she decided to try it for herself. Months in advance of the annual birthday weekend, she told her husband and adult daughter that the time had come for them to take over the birthday hosting duties. She would celebrate their birthdays with an intimate family dinner a week earlier, and, on the weekend of the expected extravaganza, she would be checking herself into a lovely little hotel a few hours away, enjoying its mineral bath and spa. Her act of rebellion was celebrated by me and all her friends. She relayed her plans to her husband and daughter calmly; she wasn't angry, she didn't yank the birthday party away from them in an act of hostility. She calmly let them know that she intended to take a little "me time" and that she wished them a fun-filled birthday weekend. And she did. And they did. All were happy with the arrangement.

Another friend, Tanis, came to terms with her need to try the Me First experiment for herself. She told me that typically her "me time" came when her husband left for sponge hockey three times a week with his friends down the street. While her husband was gone, Tanis would make dinner, oversee bath time, read nighttime books, and tuck her children into bed. After all this was done, she would then be 'rewarded' with a quiet night watching HGTV alone. This arrangement, she maintained, worked well for her. But I was unconvinced. Eventually, as we talked, she began to see that this arrangement was less "me time" and more "he time". Over the next few weeks, she came to realize that between her and her husband's busy schedules, she was never able to find a free night to go to the movies with her friends.

"I used to love to go out to dinner with my girlfriends",
Tanis confided to me. "But now, I think a night with leftover
Chinese food, in my PJs, with Netflix and the remote control
all to myself is the perfect night. What's happened to me?". I
know well that feeling of being so exhausted that the very idea
of going out with friends is laugh-out-loud ridiculous.
Exhaustion is a common by-product of the perfect
mom/perfect wife race. If your idea of "me time" sounds like
Tanis's, you may need to reconnect with your pre-mom/pre-
wife self. Who were you before you had kids? Before you got
married? What did you like to do? Why do you no longer do
the things that you used to love? If it's because you are too
tired, or too busy, you may need to re-think the way you
prioritize the demands of life. Most likely you are so far down
the bottom of the priority list that you do not even make it onto
the page. My suggestion to you? Put on your researcher's hat
and try the Me First Every Once in a While experiment.

CHAPTER 8


**Rule 8: Savour the day**

*Create joy in your home by living mindfully*


    I am not immune to the highs and lows of life. I often fall into the futile trap of chasing that ever-elusive state of joy. In today's cultural world, we have been conditioned to chase joy. We watch with envy, the fabricated utopias curated on social media of the rich and famous and the not so rich and famous. That perfect sunset enjoyed on that perfect Caribbean holiday. That perfect meal, shared with perfect friends, on that perfect night on the town. But these moments—while, joyful—are fleeting.


    What we don't see on social media are the inevitable low points of everyday life: the hefty credit card bill that follows the Caribbean holiday, or the hangover that follows mom's night out. Of course, in our heads, we know that real life is much more than the embellishments we post on Facebook and Instagram. And yet, so many of us become joy-addicts, forever chasing the next high.

Creating joy is different from chasing joy. In creating joy, we are the architects of joyful moments. And, by cultivating a life savour mindset, we can create joy each and every day, wherever we may be. Through mindful living, we can learn to summon joy, intentionally bringing this state of being to our lives, to our relationships, and to the everyday activities of living. This doesn't mean our lives are without struggle and hardship. Rather, through mindful living and the cultivation of a life savour mindset, we come to accept the struggles and hardships of real life, as they are par for the course in our shared experience of living.

Mindful living promotes a life savour mindset. In practicing mindful living, we are training ourselves to live in the present moment. But, of course, this is easier said than done. Our natural tendency is to pay only partial attention to the present state. Most of the time, we are consumed by our future and our mountain of To-Dos and chores (what will we make for dinner, what time do I need to pick up my son from hockey practice, when will I find the time to repaint my living room, and on it goes). But when we are only partially attuned to our present surroundings, we miss out on the never-ending opportunities to create joy in our life. Bringing our full attention to the everyday moments of our lives is truly the key to a healthier, happier life.

To learn how to live mindfully, we must start by practicing solitude. Some of us, more than others, struggle with the idea of being alone. These extroverts prefer to be surrounded by others, whether they be friends, colleagues, family members, strangers at the gym, or fellow patrons of a shopping mall. But solitude is a gift: it provides us with the experience of connecting to our inner selves and our surroundings. Indeed, some mindful living experts believe that solitude is the pre-requisite for true intimacy. To be truly intimate with someone else, you must learn how to be truly connected to yourself through the practice of solitude. For some of my most extroverted readers, I know this sounds like punishment, but I hope you will indulge me and try it for yourselves. And fear not, practicing solitude does not mean you need to sit idly still for hours on end. The best way I know how to practice solitude is by taking a walk on my own, fully immersed in nature.

Mindful living requires you to bring your attention to the activities of your everyday life. If you are eating lunch at your desk on a busy Monday afternoon, try closing your laptop for 10 minutes and concentrate on the tastes, smells, textures of your meal. If you are waiting in line at the grocery store after a long busy day, try taking ten deep belly breaths and notice the way your heart rate slows, your body temperature drops, and your shoulder muscles begin to loosen. No matter the activity, the first step in mindful living is to become aware of the moment and be grateful that you have recognized the opportunity to practice mindfulness.

Next, check in with yourself and take stock of your thoughts (are they on an endless loop of list-making or criticism?). Pay attention to your body. How is your posture? Are you clenching your jaw? Is your stomach in knots? Your body expresses your inner thoughts. If you notice tension in your body, simply acknowledge it and tell your body that you are safe in this moment and allow your muscles to relax.

And remember, mindful living is not your default setting; it will always be something that requires your ongoing attention and regular practice. In this way, practice does not make perfect. Non-judgmental acceptance that you will never be perfect at living mindfully is the gift of self-compassion.

Self-compassion comes from accepting ourselves and loving ourselves, not because of our achievements, but because we are simply worthy of such love. By cultivating self-compassion through the practice of mindfulness meditation, we can then turn this compassionate, non-judgmental outlook onto the people around us, including our loved ones.

By nurturing self-compassion, we are more understanding of and empathetic toward others. We can see the outburst of our husband as a misfire of his anger-response to stress, not the marker of a flawed character.

We can see the impatience of our colleague as the by-product of her need to be perfect and her struggle with self-acceptance. By cultivating self-compassion, we cultivate compassion for others. But first, it starts with an inward focus, an acceptance of ourselves through the practice of mindfulness meditation, especially those mantras that focus on loving kindness.

Through brain imaging, we now know that mindfulness meditation quiets the parts of our brains associated with self-referential thinking. Too much self-referential thinking can lead to self-absorption and self-criticism—a guaranteed path to misery and unfulfillment. Through regular practice of mindfulness meditation, we can redirect our thoughts away from this no-win thinking.

And as we do so, we become more focused on our surroundings and other people instead of being overly focused on ourselves.

Through a consistent practice of mindfulness meditation, you will notice you are able to get along better with your loved ones. Mindfulness meditation helps us to see the other person more clearly, to understand their biomechanics and stress responses. In this way, we become more empathetic and forgiving—we let go of the harsh words they might direct at us, we understand that their anger-response to stress is not personal—their negative behaviour does not become ours to absorb. Importantly, we nurture our compassionate selves, and we don't get caught up in condemning the other person who has wronged us. We don't take things so personally. We realize that much of the time, the other person's behavior, even if it's disturbing to us, isn't really about us. Rather, it's a reflection of their own struggles. This ability is called psychological flexibility.

Mindfulness meditation is a practice we must do each and every day for the rest of our lives. For most of us, it's not natural, it's not easy. But it is important. And it is the key to a healthier and happier life.

Do you practice regular exercise? No matter your preferred movement, a daily commitment to physical activity is essential to mindful living. But the point of mindful exercise is not to cultivate defined ab muscles or close the circle of your fitness app. Rather, it is to strengthen the relationship we have between our minds and our bodies. Indeed, some experts believe we are a "mind-body", not a mind and a body. If this sounds abstract, it simply means that our mind and our body are intertwined with each other; we cannot have a healthy body without a healthy mind, and vice versa.

Mindful exercise allows us the opportunity to connect our mind with our body in a way that is positive and beneficial for both. Importantly, mindful exercise is not self-critical.

If this is your natural tendency—to push yourself to beat your personal best, or to punish yourself for over-indulging in last night's dinner—you are missing the opportunity to nurture yourself. Worse, you are reinforcing the feedback loop of negative self-talk, which will always undermine your health and happiness.

If replacing self-criticism with positive self-talk seems like an unattainable goal for you, imagine how you might encourage a child who is learning a new sport or activity. Use your most loving and maternal voice. Offer encouragement and words of compassion. And remember the goal of mindful exercise: to strengthen the positive relationship between your mind and your body.

Another important way to practice mindful living is through outdoor activities. Indeed, connecting to nature is one of the simplest, yet most rewarding ways to practice living in the moment. Notwithstanding the natural benefits of soaking up the sun and breathing in fresh air, connecting with nature grounds us unlike any other mindful living activity. Whether you are walking amidst the canopy of an urban forest or climbing upward, toward the peak of a snow-capped hill, nature reminds us that we are part of something larger than ourselves. Nature also reminds us that our problems are fleeting—just as our experiences of joy are fleeting. Nature's changing seasons illustrate that nothing in life is permanent, that nothing in life is within our control. The rain will come, regardless of our golf tee time, and the blizzard will come regardless of our travel plans. But what we can come to rely on is our ability to live in the moment, to see—truly see—the beauty of nature all around us.

Are you a cup half full sort of person? Some of us believe that optimism or pessimism are inherent personality traits that are out of our control. However, while we do have differing tendencies toward optimism or pessimism, optimism can be practiced—you just have to put your mind to it. There is much research that suggests practicing optimism is a key strategy for nurturing a healthier, happier life. This makes common sense, yet we seldom put in the effort to practice optimism.  For some of us, optimism is wrongly viewed as a delusion, the mind game of fools who pretend life is a bowl of cherries. But let's put aside our personal values of optimism and strictly look at the research.

The biomechanics of our brains show us that we are largely affected by negative thoughts and negative experiences. Our brain is hard-wired to detect the negative and to avoid it at all costs—and this is a very clever survival strategy.

This is why it is our natural tendency to remember the negative moments in our life; it is our brain's way of flagging danger so that we can avoid it and survive a perilous world. But this clever survival mechanism is also the greatest enemy of personal happiness. Our ever-worried brain, doing its bit to keep us from danger or death, is pre-occupied with the negatives around us. That is why we need to train our brain to become a more positive thinker, a more optimistic operating system. To do this, we must re-frame our thinking. But before we can re-frame, we must pay attention to our inner voice by living mindfully.

To practice optimism, we first must spot our pessimistic tendencies. Only then can we re-work our thinking and find the silver lining in our situation. But this again falls into the category of easier said than done. The best way to cultivate a regular practice of optimism is through the practice of reflective journaling.

By writing about your day and your experiences, you will reveal to yourself the natural tendencies you have toward negative thinking. And by reviewing your written reflections and re-framing them through a more positive light, you will become more adept at the practice of optimism, an important ingredient in the life savour mindset. Here is an example from my own journal:

| My Reflection | My Re-frame |
|---|---|
| For two years in a row, our big Thanksgiving dinner has been canceled because of COVID-19. It's hard to sacrifice these family occasions and I am so heartsick at missing these special occasions. | For two years in a row, my family has chosen to cancel our big Thanksgiving dinner in order to keep my elderly parents safe from COVID-19. These two years have been such a struggle, but I know we are lucky to be healthy and safe. |
| Today Tony and I went to couples counseling. It is super expensive, and I am not sure it will even work. We are such different people and living together is so hard. | Today my husband and I made the decision to work together, with the help of a counselor, to resolve some of our issues. I am sure it will be a difficult process, but knowing Tony is willing to put in the work and the money to better our relationship makes me realize how committed he is to me and our family. |
| Maggie has moved out of the house in order to attend | Maggie has begun her University program and is |

University in the city. I am an empty nester now, and I miss my kid so much. I no longer know what she does each day, who she sees, what she eats, what time she goes to bed. It's hard not being as involved in her life as I once was.

living in the city. I miss her so much, but I am proud to see her becoming so independent. And I am grateful that she still wants to come home a few times each month to visit me.

When you first begin your practice of reflective journaling, don't censor yourself. If you have a tendency to find the negative in life, allow yourself to write down these thoughts. But, as you can see from my own journal entry, split your journal into two columns: your uncensored reflection, and your positive re-frame.

This template allows you to be honest with yourself so you can come to understand your natural reflection tendencies. But importantly, it provides you with the space to review and re-frame your reflection into one that has a more positive spin. By reframing your entry, you are not judging yourself for being pessimistic; rather, you are gaining insight into how you interpret your life events, and you are practicing how to view these events through a more optimistic light. Remember to be compassionate with yourself; taking the role of an observant researcher may help with this.

Once you've begun to master the art of positive re-framing, demonstrate this skill with your loved ones. When your spouse or children express their disappointment with the poor weather, which has ruined their tee time or their outing to the park, be careful not to dismiss their feelings. Let them express their disappointment, just as you allowed yourself to reflect in your journal honestly and authentically.

Then, after validating their feelings of disappointment, help them to see the positive in the situation. Remember, the silver lining doesn't have to be huge—we don't have to over-compensate for the ruined outing by planning an even better indoor outing. Rather, after validating the disappointment of our loved ones, we might simply offer them assurance that we, too, are disappointed, but that as long as we can enjoy each other's company, the day is never lost and the opportunity for joy is always present—rain or shine.

# CHAPTER 9

*Keep learning!*

My goal in writing the Zen House Rules was to offer working moms a source of information they could trust, while, at the same time, keeping the science jargon to a minimum. If your interest has been sparked by my book and you wish to delve deeper into the science of wellness, I have assembled a list of my favourites. Enjoy this reading. And remember to share what you have discovered with the women around you. The life of a working mom is hard (the understatement of the century!), but the more we learn and share with one another, the stronger we become.

*Suggested Readings:*

Finlay, B. & Finlay, J. (2019). *The Whole-Body Microbiome: How to Harness Microbes—Inside and Out—for Lifelong Health*. Douglas & McIntyre.

Johnston, T. (2021). *Children, Childhood & Childcare: A Critical Discourse Analysis*. Shore Stone Publishing.

Maté, G. (2004). *When the Body Says No: The Cost of Hidden Stress*. Knopf Canada.

Mayer, E. (2016). *The Mind-Gut Connection: How the Hidden Conversation within Our Bodies Impacts Our Mood, Our Choices, and Our Overall Health*. Harper Wave.

Nestor, J. (2020). *Breathe: The New Science of a Lost Art*. Riverhead.

Perlmutter, D. & Loberg, K. (2015). *Brain Maker: The Power of Gut Microbes to Heal and Protect Your Brain—For Life*. Little, Brown and Company.

Perlmutter, D. (2013). *Grain Brain: The Surprising Truth About Wheat, Carbs, and Sugar—Your Brain's Silent Killers*. Little, Brown and Company.

Pink, D. H. (2009). *Drive: The Surprising Truth about What Motivates Us*. Riverhead.

Rosenberg, S. (2018). *Accessing the Healing Power of the Vagus Nerve: Self-Help Exercises for Anxiety, Depression, Trauma, and Autism*. North Atlantic Books.

Siegel, D. J. (2018). *Aware: The Science and Practice of Presence*. Penguin Publishing Group.

Siegel, R. (2014). *The Science of Mindfulness: A Research-Based Path to Well-Being*. The Great Courses.

Van der Kolk, B. (2014). *The Body Keeps the Score: Brain, Mind, and Body in the Healing of Trauma*. Viking Press.

Walker, M. (2017). *Why We Sleep: Unlocking the Power of Sleep and Dreams*. Simon & Schuster.

Manufactured by Amazon.ca
Bolton, ON

25474575R00092